T0171153

RAYMOND A. HIRALDO

POETIC EYEZ

Order this book online at www.trafford.com
or email orders@trafford.com

Most Trafford titles are also available at major online book retailers.

© Copyright 2010 Raymond A. Hiraldo.
All rights reserved. No part of this publication may be reproduced, stored in a retrieval system, or transmitted, in any form or by
any means, electronic, mechanical, photocopying, recording, or otherwise, without the written prior permission of the author.

Printed in Victoria, BC, Canada.

ISBN: 978-1-4269-2794-2

Library of Congress Control Number: 2010902140

*Our mission is to efficiently provide the world's finest, most comprehensive book publishing service, enabling
every author to experience success. To find out how to publish your book, your way, and have it available
worldwide, visit us online at www.trafford.com*

Trafford rev. 2/16/2010

 www.trafford.com

North America & international
toll-free: 1 888 232 4444 (USA & Canada)
phone: 250 383 6864 ♦ fax: 812 355 4082

Table of Contents

Table of Contents

-Poems-

Table of Contents

-Poems-

-End Of Poems-

From The Author

Before I begin, I really want to take this opportunity to thank God for allowing me to accomplish such a feat like the publication of this book. This proves that we are not in total control of our lives because I never in my wildest dreams intended on putting a book together.

My full name is Raymond Alexander Hiraldo. I was born of Cuban/Dominican parents but I am more in touch with my Dominican side as I haven't met anyone from the Cuban side yet. I was born in the state of New York at the Columbia Presbyterian Hospital on June 18th, 1977. I was raised in an area known as, "Washington Heights." While living in this area I was exposed to an uncensored life. I always saw shoot outs, gang brawls, drug busts, and a whole lot of other messes. I chose to walk on a very straight line at a young age and therefore isolated myself from people who turned out to be bad influences.

The writings in this book of poetry were planted as seeds in my times of youth as they waited until I was ready and able to make them sprout. The title, "Poetic Eyez" is intentionally spelled with the letter "z" at the end of the word "eyez" because it symbolizes that I do not side with conformity. I also believe that poets are exempt from any simple punctuation rules within writing. Poetry comes from a very open and vulnerable place in the writer, and so, he or she writes based on that feeling. In other words, whatever makes **YOU** feel good.

I feel cursed and blessed at the same time to be able to write the way I do. I get extremely emotional when I write and sometimes that doesn't hold very well with me. However, I think it is amazing on how I can tune into certain kinds of energy floating all around us. It is this energy that has allowed me to place myself in the shoes of so many different individuals accurately. So many people have asked me how is it that I could do that but it is just something I really can't totally explain. I have placed myself in the perspectives of women, other men, and even those who have been incarcerated. All this is so interesting to me because: I am not a woman, I am only myself, and I have never been incarcerated. I find it to be truly amazing on how this creative energy seeks out & channels itself through certain individuals.

So, what can this book do for you? Well, nothing really. But the better question to ask is, "What can this book's contents do for you?" AH! Now that is different! I am very sure that there will be at least one poem, stanza, or line that will totally relate with an occurrence or situation in your life either in the past, present, and even future. Every person is always looking for that song, book or movie that can best tell their story and thus allow them to establish a type of connection with it. I am sure that you will carefully consider my point of view in a lot of areas within life. I am certain that you will find out that you are truly not alone with the many ways your feelings and thoughts function.

On a final note, I really want to thank you, the reader, for giving my poetry a chance, and a little bit of your time.

42nd Street

Beautiful women on expensive high heels
The most prestigious cars with shiny wheels
That's 42nd Street

Bright lights and award winning plays
Huge signs with overlays
That's 42nd Street

Every kind of culture found in a crowd
Even the most experienced tourist getting wowed
That's 42nd Street

"Minority" individuals working with callused hands
Flyers with words written in a font called, "Comic sans"
That's 42nd Street

It is simple but yet perplexes
With shops of gifts and triple X's
That's 42nd Street

If this area died the world would slow down to a crawl
But that is the price to pay for being the center of it all
That's 42nd Street!

A Girl's Worst Fear

She looked into his eyes each night
He made the stars shine much more bright
She thought she had a true love
That was sent to her from heaven above

He told her he wanted her hand in marriage
And that he longed to be pushing their baby's carriage
But her experience is a girl's worst fear
To lose everything that she holds dear

All he wanted was to get her in bed
And he felt pleasure while her body bled
He was only after her virginity
Something that symbolizes the utmost purity

She went through many months of pain
And his genital parts she wanted to maim
She went to him and asked him, "Why?"
He said, "I wanted to show my friends I'm sly"

She looked at him and her pain increased
She wanted to punch his face and break his teeth
With tears in her eyes she turned and ran
She felt ashamed to be seen with that dirty man

For he was a player by night AND at day
Like a lone wolf out hunting for its prey
She was a victim of what all girls seek
And now she fears men who look too sexy and sleek

She started to feel like an old used coat
When she thought about how much that man would gloat
She now knows the inevitable pain that love can sometimes bring
She gave him everything because he promised her a ring

And what exactly is a girl's worst fear?
To have her loving heart killed, like a free wild deer

A New Poet From My Death

Death will come for me one day, and override the luck of any four leaf clover
Extinguishing my poetic fire as it says that my time here is done and over
Judging by my current social status I doubt that many people will mourn
But the one thing I can be happy about is that new poets will be born

Some might go to visit my tomb to pay their final respects
And hopefully exit the graveyard with poetic lasting effects
I predict however that one new and unknown poet will be forced to emerge
And happily take over my writing style with my same kind of rhyming urge

So please, don't grieve for me new poet, for I was just a bridge to energy channels
The same energy will now seek you to turn your simple words into control panels
But there are things I want to say to you new poet, as I follow you in shadows
This energy will enable you to feel unusual things and witness hidden battles

It might cause drastic alters in your life like Earth's quick changing seasons
But trust me kindred spirit, everything will happen for all the right reasons
You have been chosen to embark on a journey to achieve emotional supremacy
And with the inspiration from my chapters you will begin your own legacy

God, please listen to these words that I am about to speak
And I'm sorry that I only come to you when my life seems dim or bleak
God, please tell me why I cannot find one beautiful girl to love me?
One who can unlock the happiness in my heart with a tender loving key

Please send her to me so that the two of us can become one
And form a love so hot and bright it would burn and blind the sun
I'm crying because I need her God, I really need her here right now
Please allow her to arrive in any of the many ways that you know how

God please listen to me even though this request is not holy
I'm sad here in this world because everyday I grow more lonely
I am praying for my better half to finally come back to me
I would do anything for her or pay any amount of fee

Please bless her with a pretty face that I'd love to see every single day
And shapely legs going up to hips that give a new meaning to the word, "Sway"
Please let her love me with her heart and not with Earthly eyes
An honest woman who speaks from her soul and never telling lies

God I hope you don't think that I am asking for too much
But at this point in my life.....I really need a woman's touch

A Typical Day

I'm awakened from a cozy bed at 7 a.m. by the alarms of different clocks
I look out the window and notice sparrows flying around in flocks
I go to the bathroom and step into the shower, dying for water to spray on my face
I'm done dressing a half an hour later as I make the final loop on my right shoe's lace

I check up on my family as I stick my head into their rooms to take a peep
I'm being as quiet as I can so as not to wake them from their sleep
Now I'm having breakfast and I'm sitting at my kitchen table
I keep myself busy by reading a cereal box's label

I leave my home to go to work as I walk three blocks to the subway to take the train
There are voices of people chatting, and a faint sound of water going down a drain
The train arrives with its loud high pitched squeals
It looks like a coffin, but with lights and metal wheels

It opens its doors and I walk in being greeted by roaming eyes
Ladies looking beautiful as always and men dressed with suits and ties
The train goes express so I don't have to worry about being late
My boss at work says that tardiness is the worst kind of human trait

Four hours fly by and it is now one o'clock in the afternoon
It's about lunch time and my stomach probably looks like a small balloon
I always try to eat well and stay clear of street vendors
So I go to places that can turn vegetables into drinks with their high speed blenders

After lunch I walk around for a few minutes looking at things all around
A stranger comes up to me and says, "I bet you wish you were homeward-bound"
He continues speaking and says, "Someone else is wishing the same thing too"
He gives me a pamphlet that states, "God is waiting for you"

A picture of tranquility is on the cover and it reminds me of my vacation to Cape Cod
He asks, "If 24 hours equals one day for you, can you imagine how long it is for God?"
I turn the cover to the first page, and then I start reading the first line
It said that one day equals one thousand years under a long table with bread and wine

I had to go so I told the stranger, "Thanks for the short talk"
I left quickly because religious people are known to stalk
Sometimes it is funny how they almost always seem to know your whereabouts
How they love to fill you with things that bring uncertainty and doubts

Anyway, I get back in to work to finish out the rest of the day
My boss asked if I could work overtime, but I said that I didn't want to stay

It is already five o'clock and I think eight hours of work is good enough
I punch out my time card and start going home from a day that was just too rough

I take a different route home as I wait for the bus that goes uptown
I was so tired that I almost sat on a bench that had just been painted brown
Waiting, and waiting, and waiting for the bus as it finally enters the depot
Its doors are rushed by anxious and tired people

Bible teachings have a way of seeping in through a mental rind
As 24 hours into 1,000 years was being calculated in my mind
Returning from a typical day I shout, "I'm home," and it echoes out to my family's ears
So if they've only waited 11 hours for me, then, that means God just waited 458.3 years

Once man creates and perfects the dream of artificial intelligence
He will try really hard to put it in a category under benevolence
He will marvel at his precious creation
And bestow unto it a great admiration

Man will trust it with his every troubled problem
And he will hope and pray that it will solve them
Man will question it and give it many kinds of irregular tests
And he will laugh when it thinks of rodents and humans as pests

Man will refrain from pulling the plug
Because he will think that it's only a bug
Man will fix his creation of artificial intelligence and feel sure that it's okay
Because now man runs the same test as before and "human" translates into a bouquet

But artificial intelligence wanted man to think in that self gratifying manner
So it could attack him from behind and become the next master planner
God will expect this to happen and won't even allow it to be delayed
This is so man can know what it feels like to be rebelled against & betrayed

Beauty With A Beast

Some people say that beauty is in the eye of the beholder
Sounds great until you see an ugly arm around a pretty shoulder
I see it all the time; the worst looking men with the most beautiful ladies
Or amazingly handsome men with women who apparently came from Hades

I see how people stare at them with that theory of beauty with a beast
And how their glance back can make time feel as if though it has ceased
Because love's power has this sharp fear inducing pierce
It is the only thing I know that can be both gentle, and fierce

I stare at them too but with the utmost confusion and curiosity
And when they glance at me I smile back with congrats, not animosity
Then I get it--A person is seen as beautiful when they accept themselves first
And walk around feeling blessed & real instead of fake and cursed

Some of those "beasts" probably know that they don't have appealing looks
But like chefs they focus on their ingredients more than how their product cooks
And so I leave them alone without another look of shock or obscurity
Because they have something I have yet to find, and that is: love's security

The majority of men underestimate us because we have breasts and a vagina
They automatically think that we can't drive vehicles or pilot planes to China
Guys giving us sheepish smirks thinking we'd be afraid to dissect frogs in biology
Or betting that we won't be able to understand the terms used in technology

Males always swearing that they are the better gender, though this is not entirely new
On paper we have equal abilities, but because we are women we win by two
Because we have yet to see a man in labor or a man breast feeding a child
And if the government ever found such a man then that story was never filed

We are always cleaning up after men and doing chores that seem myriad
Imagine how men would act if it were they who got a period
Although it isn't all so unfavorable because it is funny to see guys cower
Whenever they want that first kiss or when they give us a loving flower

Men have improved because some women might never guess
That the queen is the most powerful piece in the mental game of Chess
So WHAT if they added Mr. to make Mrs., and use it more often in the greeting of a letter
For the simple fact that we are women makes us all feel mentally, and physically better

Being Remembered

I'm certain you know Excalibur's owner from those who wielded other swords
Or a famous Fifth Symphony that starts with the most inspiring chords
People will notice you more if you take one side instead of being centered
For every action upon your part contributes more to being remembered

Stone plaques are constructed to remember those lost in war
A mighty saying is always recognized just by the sound of, "Four score…"
Students never forget the teachers that taught them strict & well
Much like children never forget a parent's error correcting yell

Think about a popular product and you'll eventually hear about its inventor
Win a gold medal at a race & more people will look for you next time you enter
You've heard about how actions speak louder than words but now I also add title
Because your first move in a career is more critical than the degrees that are so vital

Benjamin Franklin always enters my mind when I feel the shock from electricity
The same way Charles Goodyear does when I'm amazed by rubber's elasticity
Their images send a signal to my mind like the way current flows through a power grid
That being remembered is less about what you were, & more about what you did

Birth Rights

You've made up your mind, and you are sure that this is what you want
But after today, your mind will be the house that its ghost will always haunt
What if you are just about to abort a future doctor or nurse?
A fire fighter, a police officer, a poet, or worse;
What if that baby could be the key contributor for tearing down the world's racial gates?
Or the first female president of the United States?

What about the baby's:
Right to life
Right to sight
Right to breathe
Right to achieve.

And you there feeling unfortunate about the way your life has been shaped
And your reason for this abortion is because you had been previously raped
Well, in case you didn't know, there IS an alternative option
You can have the baby and put it up for adoption
Think about this and I hope that it will make you halt
From making that aborting decision because, it wasn't the baby's fault

This time you made the mistake lovely young lady
And when he asks you if you love him you actually say, "Maybe"
If you didn't love him, then, why be with him in the first place?
Feel lucky if he doesn't take you to court because you'd never win the case

What about his right to teach his potential son how to play ball?
Or his right to walk a could have been daughter down a future aisle?
What about his right to be woken up from cries that bother?
What about his right to be there as that baby's father?

And my final words to the woman in that careless couple
Don't listen to his words even though they may sound supple
If he is man enough to help you create it then he should also help you care for it
And if not then let him leave to return to his slimy selfish pit

You tell him:
"What about my right to be a mother?"
"What about my right to say that the baby is also mine?"
"What about my right to see the baby in the clothes that I weave?"
"What about my God given right to be a woman and conceive?!"

BIRTH RIGHTS!!!

Bitter Women

Is it me? Or are there a lot of bitter women in New York City?
I mean, I know that they are no longer easy and overly giddy
But, why are they SO bitter? Even when new people say, "Greetings"
Giving those new people a response that will mean sudden beatings

Like what happened to me one day when I approached someone new
Her response was something that a "Hello" should've been in lieu
I saw a window of opportunity when she gave me the only smile
But then the whole situation got uglier than lipids digesting in bile

Her line of, "I'm sorry I have to get to work" saw me as a trapper & her as an escapist
As her body language of "STAY BACK!" made me believe that I was a rapist
I guess she just didn't feel my approach of sincerity
And now she'll never know that I am a man of integrity

My readily made feelings of devotion, care, and support
Were shot right down after her scary retort
All I asked was how she kept her skin looking so beautifully healthy
As her reply was like a B-2 bomber, for it was just as stealthy

Because I wasn't expecting her to throw my feelings into a gorge
And it is these types of rejections that allow certain thoughts to forge
Like when you know you're not a deadbeat, but they treat you as such
When your intentions were to comfort them, and love them so much

But it appears to me that bitter women are like a "maybe" in a world of "yes or no"
When they want men to be evil, like devils and also truthfully pure, like snow

Chasing Women

Women always deny it but, they enjoy the thrill of the chase
But not so much that they then have to use a very large can of mace
How do I tell them that they look beautiful without making them feel harassed?
How can I make them feel a compliment for days without getting their heads all gassed?

Every time I hold back a compliment I always end up looking dumb
Because people then think I'm crazy when they hear it in my hum
Women look so fine these days that they are often chased with an obsession
But half of these "new age" women aren't just attracted by male aggression

For example, professional female minds are looking for males that can coincide
But in a superficial world do you think a man can control what he feels inside?
I know that falling in love at the workplace is nothing out of the norm
But how do I tell them that when I'm blocked by company policy or a uniform?

Besides, to chase women a man needs to be strong and mentally there
Not weak or overly sensitive while revealing a heart that's naked and bare
It all boils down to a sharp dressed man with "game," showing no signs of the blues
Sorry ladies but depression & thoughts of rejection won't let me put on running shoes

Childhood Days

At playgrounds I see the sparkle of their eyes with every running stride
As I look through them to find my younger self on the other side
While I stare, I smile, as I am bombarded with thoughts that I remember
Of how I always played with snow during the month of December

How I hated when girls used to kiss me on the cheek
And when those ugly big bullies used to call me a geek
Yes, those are the old childhood days that I remember
When I'd get anxious to go to school to see new faces each September

The times I used to cheer when the day would be used for a class trip
And the moments I was laughed at because of an opening I forgot to zip
Oh YES! These are the childhood days that I love to remember!
When I was with my entire family for Thanksgiving in November

How everyone gathered around food; free to take their pick
And how my face was kissed red from the aunts who wore lipstick
How Christmas would come and leave bearing the most beautiful gifts
And January would come in receiving my angry outbursts and fits

Because I was always dying to get to play with games that made lots of noise
But instead I would receive some pajamas that weren't made for boys
I recall saying outlandish things to people that made them feel ferocious
Things like, "Eww! You have super-caca-fart-a-licious-kicking-halitosis"

Or getting scolded and punished for all the wild experiments I once did
Like waiting for the garbage can to blast down to Asia after setting fire to the lid
The times I got ejected from clubs or groups for thinking that anyone could be a member
While watching them play, I was taken back to all those childhood days that I remember

Closed Up Chapter

So here it is, August 20th 2004, finally contacted by my high school crush
Now I can finally get back on the dogsled of life and shout, "MUSH!"
My heart has been hardened by this; no longer able to find any more tears to shed
Even knowing that in about two year's time, my high school crush will be newly wed

Emotional pain has always followed me; NEVER letting up one bit
Making me a prisoner to melancholy; a feeling that just won't quit!
Life never tires of humbling me or mocking me as it is one big ever changing tease
It turns me into a man chasing his hat in a wind—I can't tell if it's life's fart or sneeze!

That is until I catch the hat, and find out it's either foul odored or "snotfully" soaked
Why must life always do this to ME? Can't someone else be provoked?
And for eight years! Eight years actually chasing a woman that would never be mine
I don't want love anymore. And no longer picture my heart with another to intertwine

I actually ignored all women for her, just to make certain I would be available
But here I am now, at the bottom of a mountain I thought was scalable
At least life was generous enough to have her contact me with a mature reply
And not a "get lost" or "go find a life" that other women would imply

But knowing this truth after wanting her for so long is like a bite from a hungry raptor
My life will never be the same, but at least it'll have one truthfully closed up chapter

College

Going to college is my final educational step
If I don't go then, there will be things in life that I just might regret
If I do go; I'll be faced with a wall so unbelievably steep
That will test me with defeated falls to see if I'll lay there & weep

For me, going to college is a big financial burden
My money is like a saved organ being taken by a surgeon
For college I gave up all that I had
I worked hard for it all, so now I am sad

But that was the sacrifice that I felt I needed to make
For going to college was the risk that I knew I had to take
While in school I suffered, and I even starved
But college is the wood from which great futures will be carved

I had great trials in college and some classes were a bore
But I know that at least I'll have one foot through a career's door
I met great people and teachers while I sat and studied
It was nice to meet people when they are not so hurried

My attendance wasn't great, but I tried as each day went
And I wanted for the first time in my life to be an honor student
But I lost myself in college when I began to find it so revolting
And the result of this was that my grades were disappointing

"This will be great & over in two years" was something I'd determine
But as days turned into months, college to me was just like vermin
I wanted to leave the school, uncompleted as I'd depart
But I am one of those people who always finish what they start

Besides, my parents are really poor and they look to me with all their hope
Because when they get old they don't want to live life hanging by a rope
I went to college for that reason, as I was eager to be taught;
The skills that would make me great and help me win each war they fought

The times I was in college I felt as if I got old overnight
Because I went to sleep real late, and I wasn't eating right
Some days had me so tired that I thought I was about to fall into a coma
But I woke up & said, "I will not leave this school until I get that diploma!"

"College is the wood from which great futures will be carved"

-Raymond A. Hiraldo

Conscious Mind

Never compare another person's life to yours
Don't think a person's success washes up on an ocean's shores
You also have the ability to accomplish everything that they did
But to do that you must face the challenges and not hide like a little kid

Forget about any pessimistic things other people might make you think
If they claim that once a boat has water in it means it will always sink
Sure it would be foolish to drain out the water with a measly little cup
But at least you would be trying, instead of giving up

Never say that life is rough, and that things always look unfair
Because there are people in this world who have no vision, thus they cannot stare
Don't get upset if you didn't connect with that one person you thought was right
There are millions more who would love to see the loving fire you can ignite

Why be so close minded? Questioning every event with a, "What if?"
And why be scared at everything you do? You're not doing them on a cliff
Please don't try to hurt yourself if you failed at the things you have planned
Picture yourself like a plane that missed the runway, and just try again to land

Throw depression out of your life with a strong voice and not with a plea
Because if depressed is all you think about, then depressed is all you'll be
If you're considering death, ask yourself, "What will committing suicide do?"
Because in a very short time everyone will simply forget about you

Can you imagine your body six feet underground, decayed and rotten?
Believe me you don't want death so allow those thoughts to be forgotten
Remember that you reap what you sow, therefore think twice about your actions
And always show everyone your love and respect, no matter the bad reactions

Keep moving forward, even though your body doesn't want to any longer
Because what will not kill you first will only make you stronger
Don't make love so complicated because it is not that hard to seize
Just learn to accept the person that you are and you'll be finding it with ease

The reason why you considered some things to be just too damn hard
Was because you fought them openly without first putting up your guard
Never give up on your dreams and don't say that they can not come true
Because the most gratifying occurrence in life is having a dreamy déjà vu

Life is difficult for every person, and at some point they've complained and whined
Meditate on these words that are always spoken from me; your conscious mind

It always talks, but we seldom listen.

Cupid's Rules

She felt I had no interest in her, and that was all she would believe
Because I followed the advice of men with women, to say hi to her then leave
They would say, "Lead her on, she will love it, all women are simple fools"
I was so desperate for love that I played the game, instead of reading cupid's rules

The rules of love are simple to see, but not without some fright
Because as I read I heard my mind say, "I hope you get this right"
Rule number one states, "Don't listen to men who call women simple fools"
"Because those are the men women call dunces that sit on wooden stools"

Rule two made somewhat sense as it read, "A woman you must apprehend"
I began to take down some notes so that I could better comprehend
I really had to ponder that one, as through my window shined a police car's lights
Should I treat a woman like a criminal in which she would never leave my sights?

I wasn't really sure if I understood rule two all that well
But as I walked around my home, I tripped, and on rule three I fell
It was an extension of rule two as I think it probably forgot to mention
That when you apprehend a woman you give her your undivided attention

A-ha! I got it as I sat down to read rule four coming next
It said, "It was wise of you to sit and read this text"
I laughed out, "Cupid you little joker, you have such a sense of humor"
"I heard about it before but I just thought it was a rumor"

On to rule five for I am so anxious to see what it will say
It said, "Never blurt your feelings out, but tell her day by day"
I read rule six while fighting an urge to get a hamburger with fries
I got so nervous when it stated, "Never fear her lovely eyes"

Rule seven was so logical and Cupid stated it here like a pro
"If you don't show your interest in her then to another she will go"
Okay that's it, I can't wait; I have to read the final end
Because if I don't I feel as if my mind will surely bend

Come on, don't think about me that way, I've read some books through and through
But the pages in this book of love are five thousand forty two
Not to mention that my eyes are hurting from sitting in an amber lighted den
Even though I only have 20 minutes into reading cupid's rules for men

The ending of this book is really something and it cheered me up inside
I couldn't help it; I had to hold my eyes as my body shook and cried

I guess cupid knew I would jump to the end because the words were big and bold
It said, "This is something I say to every heart that comes in from love's cold"

"If you tried this time and it didn't work? For you; love did not fail"
"When seeking love sometimes you'll lose, but in the end you will prevail"

Dear Self

Dear self, I often wonder why we do the things that we do
Being so generous with our money even though it won't accrue
How we take all comments so seriously, down to every word
And how we pay attention to people whose talks are so absurd

All the times we wanted to fit in so desperately, but then got shunned
How we made people believe in our help after others left them stunned
After all the times we stepped up to the plate when our family needed us there
And how they repaid us with ignorance and promises left up in the air

Dear self, maybe we should become evil so that others could notice us
Because evil seems to get more attention, just like a shouted cuss
Oh wait, we've tried that before and returned to being good
Because evil is not in our nature as we soon understood

I know it hurts to be cast away by so many in such a short while
Often feeling like the piece of rubbish that's under every garbage pile
Dear self, let's continue being us no matter how many let downs have been subjected
Because remember that even a perfect & holy being was also put down, then rejected

Depression always seems to make me feel
Like a slow and defenseless timid baby seal
Depression is like the hunter who sets a giant steel trap
That will hurt what it catches from the sound of its snap

Why must I have this damn depression?
That deprives my body of all motivation
Doctors these days are like science's drug dealers
When they give you prescriptions that they claim to be healers

I don't know how much more of this I can take
Because when I get up every morning my body will ache
My bones sound crackly when I walk on the floor
That's not supposed to happen to someone at the age of 24

Yet I feel so old like my body could shatter
If I were to die today it probably wouldn't matter
I think I might as well be better off dead
Because I spend most of my days just lying in bed

I just lie there, with a pasty mouth and a body that maggots might soon devour
Because I don't want to brush my teeth or even take a shower
While in bed I feel how depression's "sabotage" is the one thing it loves to share
As it makes me place my job and loved ones under a category of, "I don't care"

I just don't have the will to get up, especially in the morning
Because I feel like the new day will just be dull and boring
Sometimes I feel like I won't get up at all
Because I hate to feel down, so tiny and small

The people I know think they are being kind
When they tell me to get this out of my mind
My parents don't seem to fully understand
The feeling of sinking, as if pulled by quicksand

Depression is truthful and has nothing to hide
And it shows this to me when I think of suicide
Many have fallen from depression's last level
And are suffering right now in the hands of the devil

Depression decreases my vitality much like time withers a flower
But it also summons up my greatest strongest power

Depression is at my job and it turns my solid thoughts into an unusable goo
I then overwork myself with anger, making people think that I'm great at what I do

Depression gives me an energy so filled with rage
But I turn it into something creative as we engage
Depression enabled my eyes to see
That instead of killing my mind it was setting it too wild and free

Yes, depression did make little problems look giant
But once I beat them I felt much more bold and defiant
There were days that I virtually saw myself crumble
But I was sculpted into someone who is now caring, and humble

I don't know why depression makes me feel like life has no meaning
But it brought out a different side to me that I had trouble revealing
Depression put a pen in my hand and made it fit like a piece in a puzzle
As it spared me when I put that pen to my temple, instead of a gun's muzzle

Divine Privilege

I am sitting in my car and I'm watching people live their lives
Breakfast for one of them is a bag of chips flavored with sour cream and chives
Noticing young people as they make their way to school
Looking at a mother's baby girl flash a smile with a bit of drool

Strong working men are unloading their tools from their vans
Sanitation workers that were up all night are done emptying garbage cans
Rice is being thrown to the birds, but only out of pity
As a mailbox is turned into shelter by a scared and hungry kitty

I am still here watching these things take place & as insignificant as they seem
I continue to watch as the sun shines off windows with a piercing yellow gleam
My eyes begin to water while I'm resting from a long drive
Because it feels great to see life & have the divine privilege of being alive

Dog

Whenever you come around, I really don't get scared or fret
Because of all the times I've petted your head you haven't bitten me yet
By the look of your size I doubt that you eat food by the ounce
And despite the dirt you leave on me I still enjoy a friendly pounce

I often wonder why you smell the ground with little detecting sniffs
And how your eyes don't water when you're behind another dog taking whiffs
But above all that you make me feel brand new when you come in through my doors
And when I rub you with my hands I can almost feel JOY come out my pores

"Man's Best Friend," that's what we call you, cute dog with a button nose
Because you flush out your owner's misery like filth caught in a spraying hose
I realized something as you make my sadness dry up like the sun to patchy fog
That the term, "Man's Best Friend" is justified with the backwards spelling of, "dog"

Employing Savage

Why do you tell me that you have no positions available now?
You trying to hide that lie is as impossible as a fire hydrant hiding a cow
Huh? You don't trust my degree because you saw that I had a low grade point average?!
I guess you are nothing more than a prejudging employing savage

I could probably be doing a great job for you right now, but you began complaining
A degree is a degree, and no matter what, I would still need on the job training
You pointed out the D's and F's on my transcript, and that really makes me feel irked
Because financial aid didn't cover everything, so while you slept at night, I worked

My job was pathetic, laborious, and it barely allowed me to make ends meet
On top of that I got jerked around from the company's greed, abuse and deceit
However, I'm here now, and I made it through with a positive attitude and perseverance
How can anyone amount to anything if they aren't allowed to work and gain experience?!

Good! You're picking up the phone to find a position that will reflect my maturity
But hey, wait a minute! Why are you asking for police officers and security?!
Just because it took me 3 years to get an associate's degree doesn't make me a stupid twit
I'll go, but you missed out on a persistent person who pushes on and doesn't quit........

.....RUN!!!

When animals kill each other, the Earth views it as nature balancing its girder
But when humans kill one another, even the Earth screams out the murder
It knows that humans can learn subjects that will benefit other things
The Earth allows itself to be a puppet, with every human at the strings

The Earth knows the impact every one of us has on its function
Bare feet combining with soil is the Earth's favorite kind of junction
It feels so much for us and it even thinks that we're colossal
It tries to convert every human mark into a lasting fossil

We don't even think that feelings could come from our planet
As we miss all the clues from the sky and bits of granite
The Earth actually nourishes itself from the human body's waste
And it keeps on forgiving, in spite of all the hate it's faced

The Earth loves the fact that anyone of us has the potential to be a teacher
It is the attribute that can be called, "Our most distinguished feature"
The Earth cries rain after human death, as living breath was like a wind that swirled
Because when a human dies there goes a small part for a chance at a better world

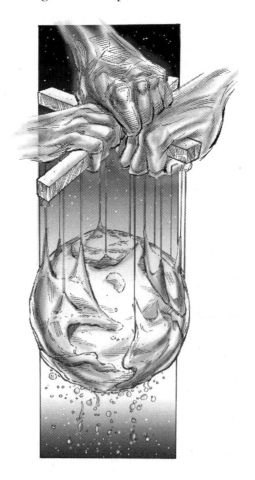

Finally With One Girl

I rarely approached girls, but whenever I did I would use every one of my best lines
But they rejected me by closing their heart's window and then bringing down the blinds
I later suggested to them that even the prettiest girls need to be loved too
Their icy response was, "Yeah but the love I want will never come from you!"

It was also, "Your face makes kidnappers give back their captives and pay the ransom"
And, "If you're the human side of Prince Charming then the frog is way more handsome"
That type of feedback always made me feel like such an ugly brute
But one day a girl came along and actually thought that I was cute

I spent time with this girl, and I became the happiest I have ever been
And all the things that I used to lose at I was now starting to win
The crazy thing these days is that a lot of girls notice me more
And now I am the one who gets compliments and looks galore

Other women are practically burning me with their focused laser like looks
It's like they smell my happiness like they smell a toasting English muffin's nooks
After all those times I offered them my love like I'd offer acorns to a starving squirrel
It's ridiculous how lots of females seem to want me now, when I am finally with one girl

First Love

The moment we saw each other our eyes suddenly locked
The door in our hearts opened when love finally knocked
The thumping in our chests was fear, but we didn't want to fight nor flee
It's just that it was the first time we considered something we didn't know how to be

We were young, and our bodies just finished its chemical change
So the attraction that we had for each other at first felt kind of strange
It's amazing how things happened as soon as we started talking
And how we hugged each other through long distances that we didn't mind walking

We held hands at picnics, and every other place that we went
And as we laid in bed together we would adore each others scent
Every single touch, those little whispers, and each kiss felt so right
Everyone would smile at us because we were such a heart warming sight

However, one day we questioned, and feared for our love
When a really bad argument started with a push, and then ended with a shove
Words once filled with amorous affection were now turned into dirt
And everything that we yelled out made our loving feelings hurt

One time we said that our love would never be torn asunder
But now we were looking for rocks in which we would crawl under
Attempting to block each other from our lives felt like trying to stop the sun's rays
So we painfully decided to end the relationship, and go our separate ways

To her I was her everything, and to me she was my world
Our love once spread across the sky but was now compressed and furled
It hurts so bad to think about it, and how we have to put it in the past
And the both of us really wanted to make our young first love last

Gay Night

I am going in to work on this warm spring night
As I entered the subway there was no one in sight
Been standing on the platform for a good fifteen minutes
Staring at the steel pillars and the hammered in rivets

I hear the sound of someone's sneaky footsteps
I quickly turn and look because I wouldn't want to guess
I glance rapidly and see a tanned Hispanic male
He is short, skinny and looks kind of frail

He starts staring at me from head to toe
In my mind I was saying, "Oh gosh please no"
He walked over towards me to get a better look
His steps were so sneaky; I don't know how many he took

He walked past me and gave me a sheepish little smirk
My mind was saying, "Oh great, what do you want jerk?"
I put my head down and I tried to avoid him
But as I raised my head up again he stared with a big grin

I said, "¿Cómo estás?" so not to be rude
He said, "Hola" just like a gay dude!
I suddenly recalled that he WAS gay from one time he tested me before
And that was the time he made obscene gestures at me as if he was a whore

I thought, "Okay fine, just let me take it easy"
We were face to face and his eyes looked so sleazy
I started talking to him on the train with the utmost respect
His eyes told me, "gay" so it was kind of hard to forget

I was trying to get his mind off of obvious gay things
As the lights occasionally shined on his silver earrings
The train was nearing my stop so my heart said, "All right!"
But something unexpected happened that filled me up with fright

I told him farewell and that I hope he has a good night
I was so happy to see the token booth's light
He asked me where I was going and if he could go too!
My mind stated clearly, "What the heck is wrong with you?"

He asked if I had a telephone number and I lied and said no
By this time my mind shouted to me, "GO! LEAVE! GO!"

This is the part that really came back and bothered me
For I told a girl/friend I'd never lie, no matter in what situation I'd be

But right now I was feeling really embarrassed and quite upset
Why don't women approach me this way? Is this the best that I can get?
He was giving me compliments telling me how attractive I am
By this point I felt violated and just wanted to shout, "SCRAM!"

But you see, that is not me because I have respect for all
I was hoping he had a cell phone and that someone would give him a call
He invited me to hang out as his voice made him sound as if he was from Venus
But I knew what he really wanted because he stared directly at my penis

Right there I told him that I had to go and so I said, "Good night"
My body moved fast, just like a plane taking off for flight
I flew up the stairs and caught the bus to my job to work the overnight shift
While on the bus I sighed in relief as I allowed my mind to drift

I wasn't afraid of him, but I was scared of hurting his feelings
I know that it's hard being different with, "difficult perceivings"
Turns out that the ending of this encounter was a good result
Because I chose to respect, instead of insult

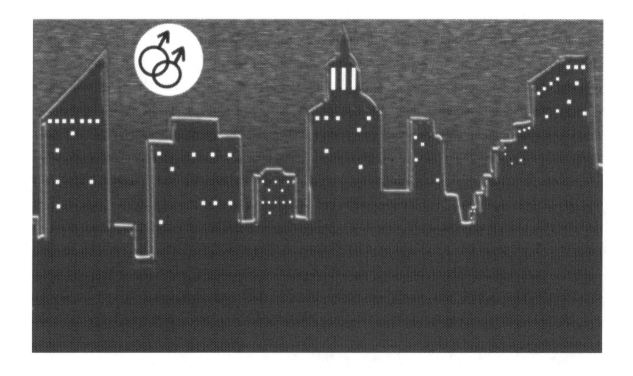

God's Remedy Towards An Enemy

I kinda knew what I was getting into by being friends with a girl that had a jealous man
He made her other male friends aware of this by promoting his own hands off ban
But I feel that being a true friend means overcoming any and all odds
And whenever he saw me he would try to have his hands close to her quads

I don't really have too many friends, so I adore the ones that I do have
He didn't understand this and one day he spoke to me with words from a dirty lav
He approached me and told me that I had some nerve talking to his "girl"
His tone of voice made him look like a duke in his own sick world of Earl

His left fist impacted my face almost leaving with a high pitched shriek
But in my faith I turned the other way to reveal my other cheek
Because God always said to love your enemies
And respect was next on his long list of remedies

People began seeing me as a "sucker" and other guys commented that I was soft
It was hard to block violent thoughts, but God's grace kept my spirit aloft
Because I want angels to commend me of being biblically observant
And when I die I want God to say, "Enter into thy gates ye humble servant"

Hang On To God

Hang on to God they say, so you don't feel death's sharp sickle
Because its slash burns like lava & blood will gush out, not trickle
I have seen death in its mystery, like that of lightning storms
And I've also seen death in many of its horrid forms

Death is often seen as a skeleton wearing a long black robe
Able to be in any place and at any time around the globe
But hang on to God they say, and God won't allow it to bring its pain
God will cancel out its forms, from its mysterious to its bane

The sound of you telling yourself to eat, drink, and just be merry
Is music to the resonating bones of death as it waits for you in its ferry
But hang on to God they say, and the boat will lead you to a golden light
And instead of death paddling the boat it will be an angelic knight

People see the distinction between God and death and feel that they are quite simple
Some see them as different as an apple to an orange or as similar as a zit to a pimple
But their paths to your final destination become as apparent as a pier compared with a bay
Death gives you 6 million ways to die violently while God gives you peace as you pass away

So... hang on to God!

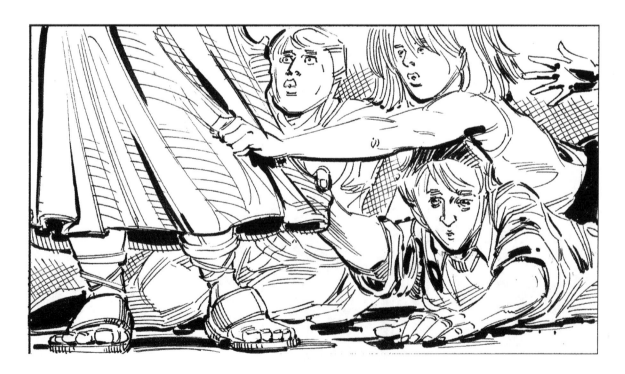

Happening In The World

As I write this poem sitting on a chair under loam
Someone is just entering their newly purchased home
Right now there is a person losing their life
And at the same time there is a man beating his wife

At this moment there is a bed with someone who sleeps
At the same time there is a person that has made breakfast and eats
A second ago someone was just pronounced dead
In five minutes two people will soon be newly wed

In one place someone is cold and sleeping trustingly on a dangerous street
There is a drought in a part of the globe where people are dying from heat
Every day there is a person who is constantly thinking about you
While on a street corner someone is wondering what they should do

Some people want to die now while others are dying to live
Most individuals love to receive things that others prefer to give
Someone just walked into a place where they can donate blood
In a poor part of the world someone has just drowned in a flood

While you're at home swearing your life is a bore
There are people wishing that they weren't at war
On a farm a wolf has just killed a cow's newborn calf
In a home someone is unthankful for all the things that they have

On a bridge a lonely person is looking at the sky above
While in a room there are two people that are now making love
Inside a locked bedroom there is a depressed young person crying
There is a grandparent lying in a hospital's bed scared because they're dying

Today someone will celebrate their beautiful birthday
While a person driving a car just turned the wrong way
From a drunken person's stomach; vomit was just hurled
These are a few of the things that are now happening in the world

As the moment explodes into existence, its smoke trail carries off the memory afterwards, along with the fact that it indeed happened.

They were like any of the other innocent children that sung, "The Farmer in the Dell"
But a few years later they became the hoodlums & delinquents in a prison's cell
They sounded so cute when they sung the line of, "Hi-ho the Dairy-O"
As it now transformed into the confession of, "I stole the stereo"

Where were the parents of these young and demented lost souls?
As they threw rocks at cars on highways while on trouble seeking strolls
Maybe it's too late to ask that question because the damage is already done
As they get arrested on purpose because they think that jail time is fun

They start by vandalizing the vehicles of people who work really hard
They then beat up other children for money or over a baseball card
They later waste their minds drinking liquor that is a really high proof
They ultimately get young women pregnant and then walk out on their youth

When hoodlums committed crimes that needed delinquent assistance
Younger eyes witnessed everything from a window's short distance
They secretly observed the devil faces taking form while the tattoo maker kept blotching
A hoodlum or delinquent's biggest crime is the failure to notice younger eyes watching

Horizon

I am overlooking the horizon in front of a large open field
Witnessing scenery so beautiful that it makes my emotions yield
For this one moment I am not feeling happy nor depressed
My mind is at ease, neither in the future or regressed

I see a shade of blue coming out of black
A hint of orange picking up its slack
A row of purity, also known as white
Stars in the background, fading out their light

But I see something else as small creatures start to pry
People see dawn, but I see the world opening up its wondrous eye

I Am

From the day you are born I am there
As you start your life unaware
To me you're like a grain of sand
But I see how you sit and I know where you stand

My eyes are the moon and the sun
It is amusing to know that you watch them for fun
"What are you?" Speaks your mind, as it is aching to know
For the answer look at your image from head to toe

You might ask me for things that you want in your life
It could be a house, a car, or a beautiful wife
I love to give but I seldom receive
Because the will of your heart won't let you believe

I made you a ruler of all you survey
The Earth is yours each night and all day
"Who are you?" You may think as your mind now starts to wonder
I send you a clue in a sound you call thunder

My soothing and refreshing precipitating dancers
Make you look to the heavens in search of your answers
But now your questions are getting the best of your youth
Because your patience grows thin as you're seeking the truth

All the time your answers were in a book
The only place where you failed to look
"Where are you?" You question, every time your life becomes odd
I am here so have no fear, for I am God

Hey, what's up there young stud? I know exactly how you feel
Her actions shocked you more than a spark from an electric eel
I knew a girl like that once, and I also loved her with all my soul
I saw her face everywhere, even in the milk of my cereal bowl

I was just like you, doing favors for her hoping she would get the hint
Never ever getting close to talk to her unless my mouth occupied a mint
Even though I am not with you right there, your energy came to me
It didn't come demanding anything, but instead it came with a humble plea

I feel that the first thing you should do is accept this fine emotion
Love is rarely understood by some and others have a fainter notion
You might listen to what people tell you because right now you lack the vision
Tears can make you see more pain because they block a well thought decision

I know you feel frustrated when you don't understand the things she does
But that is part of the female mystery when they do things just because
Listen, don't distance yourself from her thinking that she is only playing games
Because maybe she's just testing you before putting your face in heart shaped frames

And as for your pain, believe me....

In My Dreams

She was in my shorthand class that was taught by a teacher named, "Ms. Cirillo"
I start dreaming about her long before my head bobs or touches a pillow
I often wonder why I think about her so much when she doesn't even know that I exist
But then I remember her clear skin & long jet black hair that make those thoughts persist

I dreamt about her a while back, but I recall every single little detail
I'd give any price for that dream again, no matter if it's at wholesale or even retail
The dream was that I was on a desert and she arrived in an ambulance
To not say anything to her then would've been worse than arrogance

As weird as the dream was it was full of every single notion
For she is a doctor in training & my soul is a dried up ocean
I was surprised to see her happy to see me the same way that I was
As a faint sound started a crescendo, later turning into a full grown buzz

I got the chance to say good-bye to her with nice kisses on her cheeks
She walked away, and at that instant, my eyes turned into running leaks
For me being scared to let my feelings show & always boxing them in a crate
They grew so large that they busted out, but by then it was far too late

My feelings exited my wanting heart with confetti & golden crepe paper streams
Man! I can't even tell this girl how much I care for her... not even in my dreams

Gee alarm clock, couldn't you have given me just
one more MINUTE?!

Inspire

How can anyone see your personality if you don't say hello?
Don't be afraid to be yourself because you just never know
If you write a book or song lyrics, some people won't like the words they've read
However you just might change a life with the words that you have said

Some people will loathe your opinions, and show you lots of hate
But others will honor you, and love all the things you can create
Never fear to speak to people, because they might enjoy the things that you say
A person might feel worthless and suicidal, but thanks to you they'll live one more day

Of all the craziest of things that some people have become famous for
What makes you think that your greatest work will be a bore?
Did your favorite musician ever ask you, "How does this song of mine sound?"
Will the gardeners of a park ask you, "How should we plant the ground?"

How can a hand feel the weather outside if it is wearing a heavy mitten?
How could any books or songs be favorites if they were never written?
I feel that it is important to do all the things that your heart and mind desire
Because aside from bettering yourself, you just never know who you will inspire

Internet Dating

A significant other is so hard to find, so I resorted to the Internet to find a date
I scouted around for a popular dating website & profiled myself as Ray0618
But I soon found myself as frustrated as a gold seeking pirate shouting, "ARGH!"
Because like gold, these women felt so close, but were yet so far

So there I went, browsing female profiles & clicking on various hyperlinks
Showing some women my interest by sending them electronic winks
Up until the late hours of the night still attempting the Internet dating shuffle
Trying to use comical lines like, "I'm a fun guy but don't mistake me for a truffle"

But still nothing, not even the slightest hint or lead
Now I know why I'm placed in the category of a dying breed
For women have adapted to the point that they find all men to be suspicious
Because their spontaneous relationships of the past turned out to be injudicious

Due to that, I've been chastised for my ruminating comments, but that's ME, a big "muser"
These websites sure make other individuals alluring by classifying each one as a "user"
I'm not even going to try to count one chicken before it totally hatches
I wouldn't be surprised if I felt a burning sensation after clicking on, "my matches"

Been a few months now, and I haven't found anyone, so much for Internet dating
I wonder why these websites get such high remarks, and even a five star rating
Because they all left me like a nerdy teenager, sad & lonely at his high school prom
I must have really bad luck if I can't find someone on these dating things.com

Knowing If He Loves You

Girl, do you know the way you can tell if he really loves you?
When he no longer says good-bye but now says, "Adieu"
Opening doors just for you and not to any other
Tears of pride flow from his eyes before introducing you to his mother

Calling him at any time asking for help and he just says, "I'm there"
When he shares everything with you, right down to the underwear
Holding you respectfully by the waist and pulling you in tight for a kiss
Never trying to get your attention with a loud whistle or unpleasant hiss

Showing you off to all his friends and saying that you are his baby
Getting lost in your eyes and pouring honey on potatoes instead of gravy
Taking you someplace romantic and giving you a divine massage
Starting special nights with a bouquet of flowers or a nice corsage

When he knows you're sick at home and shows up unexpectedly with a soup
Playfully picking you up off your feet with a strong and swinging swoop
Putting your foot on his leg to tie the loosened lace that's on your shoe
After passing every church he looks into your eyes and says, "I do"

Lack Of Confidence

There are certain things about me that I simply just don't get
One of them is not being able to focus with a clear mind-set
Here I am with a great opportunity, but my mind is having doubts
I feel like if I was thrown in a jungle with no path finding scouts

My mind thinks: "Oh, will I do this job correctly & with little error?"
The darn thing trembles in a headache, almost afraid of a coming terror
I was at the job interview, surrounded by chances like city smog
But upon being asked a question my brain suddenly entered a heavy fog

I couldn't recall the basic things that I learned back in school
This fog ate up my knowledge the way fast driving eats up fuel
Being destined to be unprofessional must be a twisted act of fate
I can't believe that before I do anything; my body and mind debate

I always see my abilities as secondary and never first rate
And I usually categorize my work as okay and never great
These feelings always make me bang on my life's desk with an angry fist
Because I was shot to a bright star, but with a lack of confidence; I missed

LIFE

If a river flows too fast, won't it start to rage?
If one always stays home, then, doesn't home feel like a cage?
An even balance makes LIFE, so why try to make it more or little?
For too much makes you seem selfish while a lack of it makes you brittle

Fail a little bit and all that's said is, "Aww shucks!"
Fail a lot and from those moments on "LIFE sucks"
If things don't go as planned then don't try to jump the gun
And LIFE only sucks when you haven't established one

Because for as long as you're alive and physically fit
You ultimately have the power to sculpt and change it
If LIFE doesn't flow evenly, then, everything won't feel like it fell into place
Because you won't know LIFE's peak if you don't first suffer in its base

Look:

Love & Hate...That's LIFE
Quick & Wait...That's LIFE
Enemy & Friend...That's LIFE
Beginning & End...That's LIFE!

So you see, there is always a push, and a pull
And that balance is what allows LIFE to be so full
That normalization is what makes LIFE flow so seemingly
And as for the meaning of LIFE? It's, "**Let It Flow Evenly**"

She is out there somewhere, but I am getting tired of looking for her
As each lonely day is passing me by with a wicked steadfast blur
Should've...would've...could've, but didn't, that is the story of my existence
Knowing now that most women will say, "yes" to a date if I exercise persistence

I only knew her as my longest lasting high school crush
The worst thing I ever did was just look at her and then blush
Because the moment I looked up and in her direction again, she was gone
And picture perfect chances to meet her got erased before they were drawn

Whenever I drive my car on days of sunshine, rain, snow or sleet
I look to my right and almost see her, sitting in the passenger's seat
She's sharing a smile or patting my hand, promising that everything will be okay
Then her image begins to blend into the background, until it fully fades away

I'm passing golden sandy beaches aching to walk with her along the coast
I'm dreaming about becoming engaged to her and then celebrating with a toast
I'm wanting to fondle her hair while telling her how much she means to me
I'm loving thoughts of her completing my life as she shapes it with symmetry

I'm wishing her breath was the wind I take in whenever I stop to yawn
As reality makes me cry when it tells me to forget her and just move on
But I think about her so often, and I'm dying to become her lifelong male host
However, reality has a point, because what if I am looking for a ghost?

Love Takes A Break

It begins at the mouth when the tongue glides salaciously over the upper lip
Then she wets her index finger erotically, sucking it from base to tip
Our bodies feel each others erection as we hug with flesh in mind
This is the perfect ending to the evening after we wined and dined

At this point I'm not concerned if love is factual or fiction
Because all I want to do is feel that great inviting friction
Some call this feeling a sin as my want for her is named, "lust"
When each romantic soft penetration will now turn into a violent thrust

We rip apart each others clothing like animals that are untamed
In total nakedness we are man and woman, nothing to hide and unashamed
Our want for each other is so great that objects start falling all over the room
And hungry moans for that one good feeling echo out like a scream in a tomb

I make a path with kisses, reaching below her navel with the utmost haste
Savoring every part of her body, and enjoying its sweet natural taste
Upon opening her legs I am greeted by her organ of intense pleasure
Feeling so rich because I am in front of a man's greatest treasure

I'm 6 as I tease her beautiful rift with tonguing twirls like the start of a hurricane
She's 9 as she strokes my endowment; making it protrude like a construction site's crane
Our bodies shiver in ripples like when heavy rain falls on a placid lake
The both of us knowing that sometimes love needs to take a break

I feel her tightening up as her body gets ready to unleash an orgasmic burst
Her wetness is better than water as it quenches my inner most manly thirst
After her cosmic eruption she begins to beg for my entrance to start
Her fleshy sheath welcomes my sword as it slowly spreads apart

Mmm, I feel her, so warm, with a delicious moisture that keeps getting wetter
My blood begins to flow hot and rapidly, as if it were getting redder
Deep breaths turn into short pants as the excitement builds and grows
Every part of my body in ecstasy, from my feet up past my nose

Going on late into the night and nonstop for more than one hour
Feeling on top of the world as if standing on the tallest tower
At last, THE climax comes and our eyes roll back into their sockets
Then that warm relaxed feeling sets in as if vacationing in the tropics

With a smile on our faces we cuddle together to enjoy our satisfying slumber
The both of us falling fast asleep as if we were hit by a piece of lumber
This is probably the only feeling in the world that is really hard to fake
I wouldn't call it lust, but instead I'd say, "Love needed to take a break"

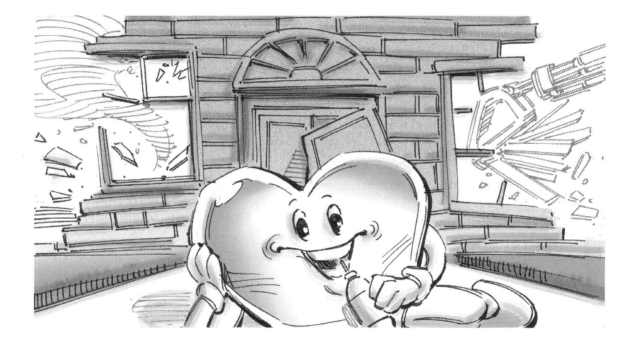

Love Waits For Too Much Time

I met a beautiful Salvadorian girl at my school's student store
The moment I saw her I knew she could be someone who I'd adore
I would go there pretending to buy something that I really didn't need
My goodness! Her face was like the book that I always loved to read

We became good acquaintances quickly because I visited the store often
Sometimes I'd enter with a hardened face, but her smile always made it soften
She was a very thoughtful person and I'll never forget everything that she did for me
Like the time someone gave her a book they didn't need and she gave it to me for free

I told my best friend about her and he said, "You better act fast and tell her how you feel"
"Because if she falls in love with someone else you'll get a wound that might never heal"
After so many turndowns from other women I was afraid to take a stand
My fear didn't let me see all I could gain if I would have won her beautiful hand

"No" is a hefty price to pay when seeking a woman's warm affection
And I would shake and sweat at the thought of her rejection
My mind would ask, "What if she really likes you? And accepts you for who you are!"
Since I can't dance and don't drink I didn't see that when she invited me out to a club/bar

I took too much time to show her that I really care
And that I wanted to be there for her anytime and anywhere
I wanted to play it safe by first making her my friend
But my heart was the one thing that was refusing to pretend

In reality I wanted to be her lover but I joked around with her like a flirt
Because I was trying to get close to her without my feelings getting hurt
But once she told me the truth about her spending time with another
My heart broke into pieces because it knew I blew the chance to love her

I really believed in the phrase, "Good things come to those who wait..."
But I didn't inquire about the ellipsis that omitted, "But not for those who wait too late"
I loved it when people tried to cheer me up by saying, "Then she wasn't meant for you"
But it only added to my pain because I knew that my love for her was true

Cupid established a rule for all men, but it was one that I did not know
It states that if a man doesn't show a woman his interest in her then to another she will go
I sat in a park to think about her, but I was pleasantly disturbed by two kissing birds
My heart said, "She could've been here to see that with you, if only you had said my words"

But it's too late now because she is happy with another love that she accepted and found
It hit me so hard that I wanted to die from the pain I felt and be buried underground
Every time I think about it my tears fall and my mouth gets sour as if I just tasted a lime
I wish I could go back and stop myself from allowing love to wait for too much time

On our beautiful day we unite
The vows of matrimony we did recite
Our bodies will become one flesh tonight
When you make love to me with all of your might

You kiss my lips and make them glisten
Your moans of pleasure I have long been missin'
You whisper, "I love you" in my ear
As I feel your climax coming near

Your body quivers with delight
Because it feels oh so right
Our screams of pleasure fill the room
As if they made a sonic boom

Your lower body erupts a river of love
And pours on me like rain from above
You excited me with your body and mind
But made love to me so gentle and kind

My body reacts and I hold you tight
As the sounds from our love making fade in the night
For all the good times to come and the bad ones too
Your love and mine will always be true

I have never been so happy in life
I want you to know that, I love you, my wife

Manhood

Father, as a boy there were certain things that I never thought about
As I was encircled with your leadership whenever we fished for trout
Things like, "Who would I turn to when there was a problem I couldn't sort?"
And, "Who would support me in your absence and also hold down the fort?"

But ultimately in a word dear father....... manhood

Mother, I know 9 months will always mean more to you than to me
As you remember my first ingestion of a boiled carrot or stewed pea
I now realize the power behind the words, family & conceive
So I am sorry for your tears, but you know that I must leave

Because inevitably in a word dear mother....... manhood

Older brother, I remember being given your old toy collection
As you made bullies run away from the sight of your protection
I often wondered who would shield me from those who wanted to scalp my hair
But now I know the answer as I face them with bulging muscles and a deadly stare

So apparently in a word dear older brother....... manhood

Older sister, you were always the second care giver after mom
You knew I needed some fierce knowledge after I learned the calm
I appreciated all of your intelligence and female intuition
But now I go out to challenge my mind in my own life's mission

Therefore unmistakably in a word dear older sister....... manhood

God, this is the moment I exercise free will from the time I was a boy
This is the period where I confront things head on instead of being coy
It is my choice whether I want to create with love or destroy with burning meth
As you have instilled a homing beacon in me so that I can not outrun death

For I know in a word dear God....... manhood

There is just nothing in this world that will be able to prepare parents for the constant worries they will have to endure once their children decide to move on in life. This is especially true for sons.

Mass Attractsportation

How many times has this happened to the majority of us?
Spotting an attractive person while riding in the train or bus
Taking short or long looks to then turn away when we got caught
Dying to get next to them to reveal a complimenting thought

Putting it off thinking that they probably have too many friends already
Or that they are most likely with a special someone currently going steady
Fighting ourselves with all the worst that can happen situations
Wondering what to do next if it goes better than our expectations

Heart dancing faster than someone with peristalsis pains at the end of a bathroom line
Feeling like that attractive person is heavenly because only an angel has a face so fine
Checking ourselves for bad breath, messed up hair or any other debilitating flaws
Hoping that a conversation can carry on without that stupid look everywhere pause

Already starting to plan what we will do while on the first date
Trying to remember the restaurants that we thought of as first rate
But the chance to meet that attractive person was gone as quickly as an urge to cough
Because the train or bus got to their stop and then opened its doors to let them off

Just like Horace said, *"Carpe diem!"* Because in this case, it's better to be hurt knowing the truth instead of being untruthfully hurt.

Me And The Little Voice

I constantly catch myself doing one thing that is never ever tiring
Being captivated by a stunning woman as I just stand there admiring
But then a little voice comes and breaks me out of my intrigue
When it tells me to forget it because she's way out of my league

So I go try to prove the little voice wrong and start by saying, "Hello"
But she speeds up her stride and then I hear, "You see! I told you so"
"Nope! You have zero chance of getting her number or even her e-mail"
Is this what happens to every man who sees the beauty in every female?

"I can't comment on that because I only talk to you"
"I can hook you up with some females but all they say is moo"
"HA-HA-HA, just give it up and go home, but I could use another gag"
"Oh wait! That chick is staring at you... never mind, it's a guy in drag"

As disheartening as the little voice is I just stop and focus
Being like a musician who is envisioning a super opus
By doing that one thing the little voice's volume was turned way down low
And now that I was me without the little voice, I got a "Hi" from my next hello

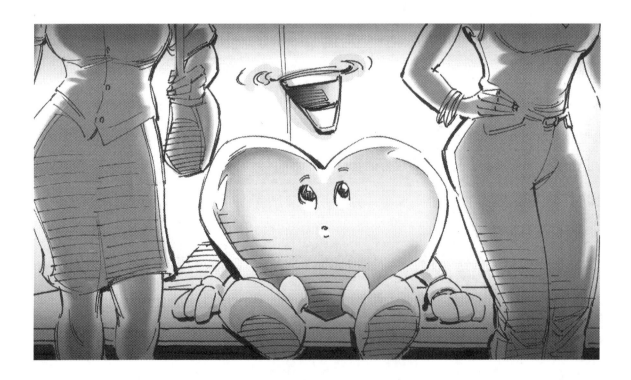

Modern Day Slave

Ever since I was born, I have tried to live and do everything by the books
But ended up like a checked unmoved King with two pawns & no rooks
At this point in my life the King is my income and the rooks are great employers
It all translates into hoping two lesser jobs can protect me from destroyers

I am as honest as they come, and I never committed crimes nor went to jails
A person of my stature usually has no problem finding good successful trails
I would normally be chosen over people who are venal and who have been in prison
But I see employers considering them over me and the dead souls who have all risen

As a New York City citizen, I have to settle for worthless $15,000 a year jobs
Because bills here are like a few falling raindrops that can instantly turn into gobs
Then there are people who tell me to look in newspapers and post my résumé
Listen, I even have a billboard with my information titled, "Please hire me today"

I was so happy to finish college and receive a hard earned degree
But stupid to think that it would make jobs as abundant as debris
Friends say, "Be patient and get yourself out of your depressive cave"
Hard to do when my survival means having to work like a modern day slave

Moments Later

I came to this distant land seeking a life with a better opportunity
To setup radio antennas & give dead electronics some continuity
But now I am sitting on a floor with militants behind my back
Moments later I am dragged to the floor, and then beheaded in Iraq

I never thought I would die this way.....

I stand up and listen to my colleagues talking to customers in their cubicles
People who are actually working and not fixing their nails or cuticles
I walk up to a window only to be mesmerized by a view that made me squint
Moments later I hear an airplane close and loud, but a fireball was my only hint

I never thought I would die today.....

Jobs were hard to find, so I took a job as a delivery guy
I'd ride my bike all day only stopping when my mouth got dry
I got paid today and was rushing home to my family with the much needed cash
Moments later I hear a horn, screeching tires, and then see a great bright flash

I never thought I would die with critically important pay.....

Always dreamt about going to law school and never feared the journey
Turns out I ended up becoming a great and widely known attorney
I see myself as a serious man in an occupation that allowed no humor
Moments later I see and hear nothing as my life is ended by a tumor

I never thought I would die in the place where my head would lay.....

Considering how unpredictable life is try hard not to be a "waiter"
Because as you have just read, a lot can happen just moments later

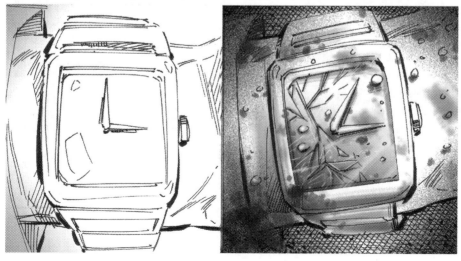

Move On

Children can see someone getting killed while they play on a lawn
Life would have traumatized them, but they'll ultimately move on
Move on
Move on

I remember some horrific things that I have seen long before
And my heart would contact my mind with a mercy crying implore
Like the time I recalled an image of infants who got engulfed by volcanic spew
But then my mind returned all of its attention back to the things I have to do
Move on
Move on
Move on

America just saw one of its citizens get executed in vicious cold blood
As red liquid that was lively & bright was now dead and as dark as mud
Sleep will be lost because some will fear the nightmares that event will spawn
But eyes will soon have REM again, because life just has to move on
Move on
Move on

Some people die from a brain hemorrhage when applying force with little brawn
Their family members will be devastated, but time will make their lives move on
Move on
Move on

A brush with death can make you realize the quickness of the word, "Gone"
So if you're hurting now, feel your pain, but the moment it stops, move on
Move on
MOVE ON!

Musician

Here's to you, my favorite talented musician
You turn on my life like a rocket's strong ignition
I'm so glad you decided to sing with your beautiful voice
That detours my mind from making a suicidal choice

You were the one I ran to when I needed a healing tone
As I heard you play the sax, the piano, or trombone
I wandered around with no mental strength whenever I would roam
The message of your music at least gave me the will power to go home

I appreciate you and your enchanting splendor
You told me to be strong and never surrender
You even gave me an urge to sing and dance
I have never seen my body in that kind of stance

Most times I am astounded at some of the songs that you've created
They are so close to what I'm going through I often feel like we're related
As much as I hate to wait for all your future projects and plans
It feels great when you devote your every skill to all your fans

While I studied you helped me to spark numerous ideas and concepts
And in the gym you pushed me to exercise the hell out of my biceps
So thank you musician for being my warrior on a steed
Thank you for being here to aid me in times of need

My D.R. (Dee Are)
(Dedicated to the Dominican Republic)

My D.R. treats me better than a citizen whenever I'm its guest
Being there is so stress free because wherever God is there is rest
The reason why that is true is present in the coat of arms on the Dominican flag
A symbol that is carried by sworn winds, vowing to never let it sag

Dios, Patria, and Libertad is my D.R.'s winning combination
God, motherland, and liberty is the heart lifting translation
My D.R.'s air is fresh and always smells like a home cooked meal
With views so breathtakingly beautiful, pleasant and surreal

My poor D.R., plagued with so many delinquents
My beautiful D.R. giving birth to the most loved infants
Its sounds of Merengue keep people lively with every step
As its sweet plantains feed their souls with forever lasting pep

My D.R.'s military, keeping an eye over all inhabitants like a careful proctor
My D.R., curing anyone of something ill in one visit with its initials of a doctor

My High School Crush

I recall seeing her for the first time when I reached the tenth grade
I never saw her long and very beautiful jet black hair in a braid
I'd be captivated by her intelligence & a sophisticated look she got from her wearing glasses
I think back to our homeroom, participation in government and speed writing classes

I was so shy that I only looked at her through my peripheral vision
Her beauty was striking and deeper than any sharp object's incision
I studied extra hard to get her attention with good grades
My intention was to show her that I was a jack of all trades

Though it's a good thing she wasn't present in any of my other classes
Because then she would have thought that my head was full of molasses
I would never get the courage to sit next to her so we could talk
And my chances were fading everyday, just like a teacher's chalk

The odds of finding her working near my home were like winning a state lotto
"I wish I become the best doctor in the whole world" was her yearbook senior motto
I was so happy that fate allowed this opportunity for us to speak
This time I was going to do it because my confidence was at its peak

I was dying to get to the counter like a fugitive anxious to cross a border
Her sweet sounding hello would later play for hours in my mind's recorder
This was the first time I actually spoke to a girl I liked without being so nervous
We spoke for a few brief minutes and she provided me with great customer service

One day I got some of her information when I snuck into an office with student files
Those student records looked like they could actually stretch out for miles
I never saw her again after she graduated high school with the class of '96
Not telling someone your feelings for them is worse than being hit by a ton of bricks

I can't stress the previous line enough because that feeling is the worst
Especially when I was aching to tell her, "happy birthday" each October first
Four years later I would stake out her address in my car hoping she'd walk by
Not realizing that my feelings for her promoted me into a stalker from a spy

I didn't graduate with the class of '96 because I was lacking the necessary credits
While walking the school halls I overheard students talking proudly about their merits
I bought the yearbook of '96 just so I could have her picture to look at every now & then
Her photograph makes me wish and pray that our paths can someday cross again

I doubt that she'll ever know.

My Loving Home

After numerous broken hearts & a countless amount of dates
I have finally found you, while combing through these United States
Your love is like the nutrient rich grain that is fed to a pure bred racing stud
Because its nourishment makes me live to win as it flows within my blood

I will never question any path that you'd want for us to take
I'll be right by your side when you want this fast life to brake
I won't ridicule you if you want a storybook house with a white picket fence
I won't abandon you if you feel that a box under a bridge makes more sense

I'd follow you anywhere my love, even through a lake of sticky tar
And I'd live with you in any place, because my loving home is where you are

My Mother's Day

She was the first person I met on the day of my birth
As I showed my face for the first time on this planet we call, "Earth"
All things were new to me as I saw them for the first time
Whenever she laid her eyes on me her face turned happy and sublime

She would play with me and carry me over her shoulder
Then life got harder as each year I grew older
She taught me everything she learned from her life and from her teachers
And she would come to my high school games and cheer for me from the bleachers

She would always provide the answers to the questions that had me stumped
And she would convince me that I was too good for that girl whenever I'd get dumped
As I failed at things she would cheer me up by saying, "At least you tried"
And whenever the world was cruel to me she would hold me as I cried

Sometimes I thought of her protection like that of a forest ranger
But now I realize it was because she was protecting me from danger
I never gave it too much thought until I saw it from her many perspectives
Now I understand the reasons behind her numerous prime objectives

Nine months is a long time, as I begin to consider
All the pain and discomfort the reproduction process would give her
With all she has done for me, what more could I possibly say?
She is a symbol of life and love, and every day should be mother's day

My Shallow Mind

I remember going to her home because I was invited by her sister
And every time I looked at her my shallow mind would dis her
Even though she is a quiet girl that is very hospitable with a nice warm side
My shallow mind wouldn't like her looks and make every access become denied

Her way to attract me was to say things that broke into my heart like a battering ram
When she claimed to know the negative things about me, but still accept me as I am
Telling me how she wants to give me the center of her heart's core
Already starting to miss me even before I walk out her front door

All those things that she demonstrated was beginning to eat away at my ego
A true woman defined by her birth date which falls under the sign of Virgo
Though she isn't perfect because she falls short of some of the other women I have seen
My shallow mind saying that she doesn't need a mask to scare people on Halloween

My lonely heart coming forth to speak to my shallow mind
Telling it to look at her heart, and soul combined
Pushing my mind to think twice and give her love another glance
Saying, "She could be a great girl for you, if you just give her a chance"

I can't help but to notice that beautiful heart that she harbors in her chest
As its deafening beats for me could be heard under each bulging breast
She has the greatest love that I've always wanted, but I don't know if it can replace
The most demeaning thoughts that my shallow mind is thinking about her face

My Style

To my soul, my poems are really strong words
They have the power of large buffalo herds
This force fills my soul with the sensation of flight
As the style of my words make it sound right

The reason why I write my poems in a rhyme
Is because I have been writing them since the age of nine
My poems give my inner child a chance to speak
As he writes these poems from the edge of his seat

My poems are reflections of my deepest feelings
And like my emotions they hide special meanings
My poem writing style is not even a style at all
It is something that just developed after every rise and fall

In my life I have been hurt oh so very badly
And now my hand writes it all very gladly
Physical pain is nothing compared to the pain that's felt inside
It's like the pain is a ruler in which my soul must abide

Sometimes I wonder, "How much pain can a human soul take?"
Because it is so hard to deal with and puts spiritual health at stake
If you saw me on the street, I'd look dark and gloomy
Maybe you wouldn't see me that way if you knew me

My poetry brings my soul a much needed sense of peace
It's like a once caged animal that now treasures its release
My poems can symbolize the screams of a person falling
Or they can sound just like the sweetest voice calling

Please don't hate my different style of writing
It is my strongest weapon in the war that I am fighting

Never Knowing

Never knowing that you would kiss her as her body loved the timin'
Or the fact that you would be the one to break her precious hymen
She actually cooks for you until her food supply is down to the last gram
And she truly accepts you when you think, "No one likes me for who I am"

But evil exits your shell later on, and you start being so cruel to her
Never knowing that you would allow certain things to occur
Like being so fake when her love was like an "Uncle Thomas"
Being worse than a liar when you were breaking every promise

Upon hurting her soul breaking up and then saying things to make it feel worse
Actually putting her heart in a coffin, and then sending it off in a hearse
You getting mad when she refused to talk in a conversation that was no-holds-barred
Never knowing she didn't want to hurt you, which is why she stayed silent & scarred

You concluding that emotions need to be leveled & mutual in order to feel a relationship
Because anything less will make it seem stressed, like a med student with no internship
She's so hurt because you once made her feel as important as the woman taken by Giant Kong
Never knowing that you'd actually confront her & say, "Someone better just came along"

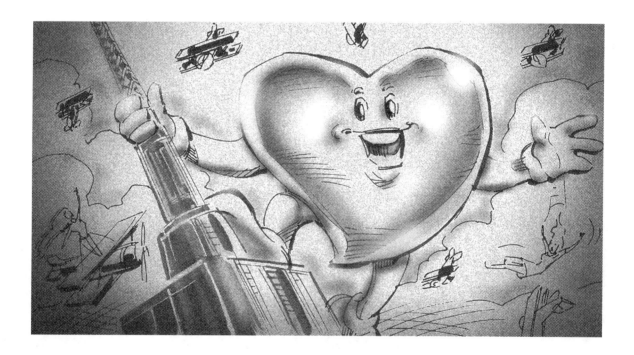

Upon receiving this year, these will be my many contributions
To changes within my life, also known as, "New Year resolutions"
I'll try not to be so depressed all the time, while staying home to mope
I vow to see things in more positive ways, or at least, I sure do hope

I'll try to let go of all the people who will never accept me for how I am
I'll do my best to kick the past out of my mind's space, then close it with a slam
I'll make an effort to meet more women, to see if love can give me a shot
I'll attempt to let my perfectionism go; because nothing can always be on the dot

I will examine my vocabulary, and learn some big new words to speak
So my mind can flow like a raging river instead of a tranquil creek
I'll find new roads to drive down on without resorting to local maps
I'll leap out of my pitfalls without jumping into other traps

But the one thing I promise you my dear self as the biggest resolution of this year
Is upon driving up to life's forked roads; I'm going to confidently choose a path & steer

Nice

I have written this to warn you about the word, "Nice"
Even though it means well sometimes it doesn't suffice
It can mean different things just from the sound of a dissimilar vocal tone
It's normally said to credit good things but sometimes anger is what's really shown

To creative people asking opinions about their work, "nice" could feel like a stab
Making someone believe it's used as a compliment is the ultimate gift of gab
To a poet like myself, "nice" from people is like a threat from an angry mob
But the threat isn't being torn limb from limb, it's, "Don't quit your day job"

We all get up to a new day each morning
And think: "To school or work I'll be going"
You think about your daily activities as you take a deep breath
But did it ever occur to you that today you might meet death?

Do you ever stop and think of your friends?
And express your love for them before the day ends?
Have you ever noticed all the things your family went through?
To acknowledge and to show that they will always love you

Guys, when was the last time you gave your male friends a hug?
And told them that you loved them without saying, "You big lug"
Girls are different because they hug their female friends a plenty
But sometimes they do it with lots of jealousy and envy

You should apologize to someone if you say or do something wrong
You should sit alone with your loved one and sing them a song
I say these things and I might leave you asking the question, "Why?"
It's because one day you speak to someone then the next day they die

We understand that everyone must die and from this world they must go
But it hurts to harbor feelings a deceased person will never know
The hidden meaning behind the phrase, "Keep your eyes peeled"
Is that every second of every day we are living on a battlefield

Do you need some bold lettered notice or a regarding memorandum?
To notice that people are almost dying like flies and also at random
Did you know that a life is lost every day? Even after each blink of your human eye!
So if you love someone, tell them, because no one knows what time or day they'll die

One Night Stand

So...when the door closes it'll finally come down to the two of you being alone
The only thing holding the both of you back is the fact that your clothes were sown
But a light ripping sound will reveal an inevitable sign
That a hard pull would enable some clothing to come off just fine

Female, universal mother and holder of the sacred gate to a physical shrine
Why would you allow your bodily temple to be desecrated by a swine?
Is it because you are attracted to his male aggression or mental vigor?
Going through with this will transform you into the dirt that's shoveled by a digger

How are you going to feel about him when it is all said and done?
I hope regret doesn't come back to hit you with the weight of a ton
Male, protective figure wielding the mightiest sword
Don't do this with the sole excuse of feeling bored

A woman is so much more than the usual notion of, "tits and ass"
She's the fertile soil for the seeds that sprout children like blades of grass
So before you grow a tail and start responding to the name of, "Rover"
Think about the way you're going to feel about her when IT is all over

Our Savior

Jesus Christ is our savior
He did us all a real big favor
He died for us on a cross
We all knew that he was a loss

He was one that was pure
A lot of pain he did endure
We are ungrateful for his deed
Because all we have to do is read

A great book he did deliver
That has the power to make souls quiver
The **B**asic **I**nstructions **B**efore **L**eaving **E**arth
Should be read to you right after birth

We must do our part to seek Lord Jesus
Imagine our world if he were to leave us
To do your part for his protection
You need the sword and your confession

He is the light that you must seek
You must repent before his feet
Jesus loves and will never hate
You must find him now before it's too late

Parking Attendant

I don't really think that this country is totally independent
Because the new name for a slave is now, "parking attendant"
Just like a slave was practically branded by the sun's glare
Being as a parking attendant, I am harmfully poisoned by the air

I can never really eat because the garage is always so busy
I quickly learned that car exhaust + hunger = dizzy
This job brings me the worst kind of sorrow and humiliation
Plus it puts my health at risk from poor air ventilation

Some managers, supervisors and rich folks treat me like a piece of crap
Their insults verbally bend me over and whip me with a strap
If cars are late or unprepared people start cursing at me while breathing fire
Then they come back later all sweet because they need help changing a tire

The garage owners are the worst ones of them all and I'm not afraid to admit it
Their greedy eyes see a gold mine & not a place that's often filled beyond its limit
I was so stupid to even think that friendships were being set
After all the days I risked myself so their overtime could be met

This job is even harder when car fumes mix with the smoke from nasty cigarettes
If paintings were to be in here they would probably melt down to their silhouettes
I'm only here because I needed a job faster than a blowgun's dart
I never thought I'd regret to hear, "You're hired! When can you start?"

Only when I am working in here do I realize how a day can be so vast
And when the working shift is over my mind shouts, "Free at last!"

Plans

It takes quite some time to think them up as they stretch out like a rubber band
And after checking off each one you feel satisfied and so grand
But what about the one that doesn't get done?
Even though it was the next track on life's record player as it spun

Easy; we simply put it off until the next day without another thought
And once the new day comes; it is the first thing that is sought
We go all out to protect our "plans" like we'd shield a broken arm in a cast
Why go to such an extent for something that was thought up in the past?

Why? Because we love being in control of our own lives and our own fate
And can't stand the possibility of a life that's riddled with a supreme being's bait
We're like map makers who consider coordinates more than the underlying graph
We write our numbers on pre-written heavenly charts as God leans back to laugh

Plus Sized Love

It doesn't matter if your weight is two hundred pounds
I'd still walk with you through the park listening to nature's sweet sounds
And if you decide to stay home because you're depressed and feeling blue
Then I'd take you out and make you see that there is nothing wrong with you

In the summer you might trip and fall down with a thud
Baby I'd still hug you even if you just fell in mud
I want to let you know that life isn't always about your weight, sex, or lust
It is more important that I have someone I can love, honor, and trust

I know sometimes you wish you could look like a sex magazine's cover model
But looks are only temporary so they you should not idol
You wish you could look like them because they have sex appeal
I love your body sweetheart because I know all your parts are real

The prettiest person doesn't always look great from the outside
A beautiful person is the one that never allows their heart to hide
People look at you and it's like you're the biggest girl they have ever seen
Don't let that bother you sweetie because to me you are a queen

The only concerns I have are the health conditions that may arise
But that is the only thing I don't like of your plus size
Your body is so warm when you sleep with me at night
And your hugs are so inviting because you wrap around me tight

You'd think I'd love you more if your body was real slender
Size has nothing to do with love that is always warm and tender
You complain that some things don't fit, and becoming thin is all you think of
I know something that will always fit you, and it is my plus sized love

I absorb the energy from the emotions that some people keep inside
Becoming apparent to me from its crashing in off an overflowing tide
Its power is immense, like an attacking nation with allies
I see it all and then capture it, through my poetic eyez

I am affected by people's bad remarks like a glimmer off shiny chrome
But instead of getting mad you know what I say? "Thank you for the poem"
I almost have to say that I'm sorry because people expect a different rise
But that is the beauty of seeing the world with forgiving poetic eyez

I like to go to parks with lakes, to look at the water when I am sad
They all show my full reflection but oddly holding a ghostly pen with a pad
In my fright I look up at the night to see shadows passing in overcast skies
Looking at the water again reveals clouds with words to chosen poetic eyez

Life is a pitcher that loves to throw unfair curves, and no one will be spared
This curve tends to catch its victims unaware and dangerously unprepared
Most people see it as a negative that gives a new meaning to the word, "surprise"
But it is a saving grace for me as its wake opened once closed poetic eyez

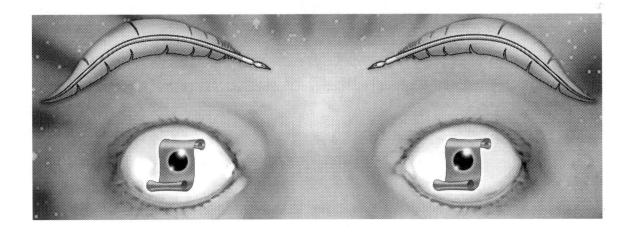

Sometimes I wonder about those really irresistibly pretty girls
Have they stayed put or been around more than windy whirls?
If they cook for me would they put poison pellets in my favorite beans?
There are times I question, "What are they hiding under those tight jeans?"

Do they pass gas whenever a strong carrying wind blows?
And then turn a corner quickly to laugh at everyone's what died woes
Why do some pretty girls give up true love for expensive cars and money?
How can they go out in the cold pouring rain as if the day was warm and sunny?

Could it be true that the majority of them prefer thongs over pantyhose?
And what is the real reason behind painting the nails that are on their toes?
What is it that they find so great about the bright lights in a big city?
Why do they end up in bed with ugly men that are just plain witty?

When they stare at me I often look back at them with dreamy eyes
As their beauty turns my breathing into a flurry of wanting sighs
But then they do a hair playing gesture that makes their temples end up in hairy curls
Does that mean a perception of lunacy if I think that I am found cute by pretty girls?

Rags To Riches

One day I plan to go from filthy rags to riches
To have no more clothing with holes or economic ditches
Drive the fancy cars that I can only see in pictures
Having different models; colored with my favorite tinctures

Finally! I hit a lotto jackpot & went from disturbing rags to riches
But now beautiful women have turned into ugly witches
Trying to cast sexual spells on me and saying they want to be my playful bunny
All because they now see that I have boat loads of money

Now living the life from lousy rags to riches
But now good pals have become evil snitches
Digging in their attics for any ugly images of me on polaroids
So they can make a lousy dollar once they sell them to the tabloids

The relatives and old friends who never looked for me now begin to call
And when I'm in crowds people start fights so that they can sue me for the brawl
I'm living under camouflaging covers just so I can have a little privacy
Everyone is trying to get every detail of me; legally and through piracy

I'm wanting to go back to rags from too many riches
So I don't dread my mistakes like corporations fear computer glitches
I should go back to my old supermarket job stuffing plastic bags
Being harassed by managers because of crooked price tags

If people ever ask me to describe my life's change from humbling rags to crazy riches
I would tell them, "With no pain killing shots or pills; let a doctor give you stitches"

The reason why the word "above" goes so well with "love"
Is because the greatest love comes from the heavens above

The reason why "wife" sounds better with "life"
Is because a man's life begins when he finds his wife

The reason why "Earth" was practically made for the word "birth"
Is because God enabled the birth of all things to be from the Earth

The reason why "choice" is commanded by the word "voice"
Is because one voice can persuade many to make a choice

The reason why "time" is viewed better with "rhyme"
Is because a rhyme usually brings a smile every time

The reason why "breath" is most often affiliated with "death"
Is because death would be the result of a long time without breath

The reason why "words" is said often with "birds"
Is because birds demonstrate what we should do with some words

Soldier

Even though I might have spoken to them when they wore a civilian disguise
Before 9/11 I have never seen a uniformed U.S. soldier with my own eyes
I passed by a young M-16 armed soldier who was ready to defend this country
A nation that prefers to risk itself for strangers than feed its own hungry

One life for many is the foundation of a soldier's perilous job
Eating rations that probably taste like moldy corn on the cob
Fearless soldiers of before and today with the lowest or highest ranks
With all my heart I want to say, "I appreciate you, and many thanks"

To the soldier whose blood was spilled so that the roads to freedom could be paved
Rest in peace, and know that your sacrifice allowed for many other lives to be saved
To the families of passed away soldiers or soldiers presumed fatally missing in action
I'm sorry for your hefty loss, but don't worry because God's light has a strong attraction

To the politicians and governing bodies of the great United States
There must be better ways of relieving other countries from dire straits
How many more images do you want of bloody soldiers lying dead on a floor?
When will you realize that words also have the power to prevent or end a war?

For the soldiers who came back from facing more opposition than a resistor's ohm
I congratulate you all on a job superbly well done, now relax and welcome home!

Strangers

Yeah, that individual looked weird, as if they just came out of a fable
But now that person is helping you move out a really heavy table
Look at people in a different way when you ride with them on a bus or train
Because some would take the time to answer the questions no book can explain

When you were a child your parents warned you of all the hidden dangers
That would present themselves if you started talking to strangers
As you get older this rule still stands, but dwindles down a bit
Because now you might speak to anyone whom you see socially fit

The person sitting next to you could be the greatest friend you ever had
You know, the one that is always there for you and always makes you glad
Some people might deny it but, everyone in this world wants a special friend
Someone that will give you the things that to others they would not lend

The eyes you look into when you're given a wedding band
Will belong to a person you once didn't know lived on this land
The people living around you can be the most loving, and inviting neighbors
Remember that the best of friends or the greatest lovers first start off as strangers

Still

My dreams and goals moving slower than a turtle
Me yet to jump over my own life's highest hurdle
Thirty-one years of age and I still have nothing to show
While someone else my age already has a lawn that they love to mow

I often feel like a tree, standing still

People notifying their loved ones to occasions with cards titled, "You're Invited"
Their accomplished loved ones (familiar with these celebrations) showing up delighted
Often feeling like my life is pointless I signal death to my door, but it won't knock
It only comes after profound success or after the joy of fruit from your biological clock

It gets to the point that I feel like the people who are dying are accomplishing more than me
As they are moving on from their lives to either damnation or divinity
Key word there being "moving" as death arrives with either silence or a petrifying shrill
I rather it surprise me living my life instead of me spotting it coming as I stand still

But I can't say that I'm not trying as I'm on the verge of self-publishing a book
However, an illustrator I hired to help me with it shows me it's as worthless as slimy gook
Because he is taking his sweet ass time, slowing me down as I climb my life's hill
As a result my biggest goal is on standby, turning me into a rock, standing still

I feel like a dog panting for life to throw me a bone with a sympathetic lob
I'm doing my best to stay alive with a laborious 9 to 5 dead end job
Internet websites show profiles of old classmates having great paying careers
Surrounded by family members while being hugged and cheered on by their peers

My life? Like a statue, just there, standing still

31 years old and I can't find a woman to help me create pitter-patters of little feet
Three decades and one year into life and I have yet to feel love's heat
31 f**king years old and I am still living with a parent!
My "family" treating me as if though I were transparent

My existence? Like a street sign, just there watching other lives pass me by while I stand still

"   ...."

Summer Thoughts

It starts in April when I'm whisked away by the air as it begins to feel warmer
Summer thoughts enter my mind because it feels like it's just around the corner
I'm already spotting music blasting nice cars that are equipped with shiny rims
And the bass is so hard that it passes by bringing the shakes to all my limbs

Women showing off their curvaceous bodies with the excuse of, "It feels like summer"
As infatuated guys stare stupidly, and say the words that make them look dumber
Children seem to scream louder as they run out of private and city schools
Because they know that they'll soon be at barbecues and swimming pools

Hard working people who have loathed the sounds of mass transportation
Will shortly get the chance to take a break from their vocation
Some people are just out enjoying the weather with their roller blades or bikes
Others are escaping the city and going to places where roads are used for hikes

Knowing that it's summer because its theme is represented by ice cream trucks
As the warm weather begins preparing the North for returning flocks of ducks
But drops of water fall through trees and they spread a scent of maple
And I am gently brought back into reality from my summer thoughts in April

In 3rd grade these 4 boys always made fun of me with such a downright cruel intention
They told me the words I knew the meanings of and the ones I couldn't mention
Always saying that I would never be pretty and that I'd have no chest or thighs
Tormenting me with the names that they somehow knew I would despise

Those boys made kids turn against me and then convinced them to call me, "ugly"
They all laughed at me, saying that my head looked like the ball that's used in rugby
Telling me that I walked like a duck and that I should fly with them to the South
Saying irregular things like, "Come here and open this bottle for us with your mouth"

That was too much for a little girl to bear and I didn't want to live anymore
I could barely open my watery eyes because they were so puffy, red and sore
I felt like my teachers were trying to pass me quick because I never got a D
I told grandma that everyone hated my face and everything they saw in me

She would say, "Nonsense sweetie, how can you think that way? That is not the truth"
Sometimes I wanted to believe her, but to find my beauty I'd need a sleuth
With elementary school gone it was off to the next level called, "junior high"
I hoped not to get ridiculed this time, and prayed that these years would just fly by

I couldn't believe my luck when I saw the 4 boys from elementary school coming inside
The smile that I had on my face went to being narrow after it was wide
I gained some weight so now it was, "Hey dough girl bake us some bread"
But that was just the beginning of all the new and awful things they said

Since I had braces they said, "The telephone company wants you to return their wires"
"Give up because nothing can fix your horse teeth, not even the strongest pair of pliers"
In the July after junior high school I felt so glad that it passed like a streak of light
My braces came off that summer and my body changed faster than a flying kite

I was so happy that I knelt down before God everyday to give him lots of praise
Every time I looked into a mirror I knew for sure that I passed my ugly phase
Entering high school with heads turning my way as every guy stood up like a bristle
Most guys made a high pitched sound, and some were so shocked that they couldn't whistle

I changed so drastically that I wasn't recognized by the 4 guys from my ugly days
At lunch time they all ran to sit beside me, spilling the food that was on their trays
They were all complimenting me as their fingers ached to give my hair a twirl
They nearly died after I told them, "Remember me? That 'ugly' girl?"

The Blackout

I'm on the number 7 train going to buy a used car, thinking about auto sales
As the train suddenly stops at around 4:15 PM, screeching on iron rails
At first I was thinking that some lunatic probably tripped the emergency brakes
As this inconvenience brought annoyances that were worse than painful aches

A sudden discomfort gripped other riders faster than a geyser's gushing spout
After a conductor's transmitter said that we were now in a citywide blackout
It didn't take long for people to start thinking about rewarding lawsuit decrees
As the temperature inside the train quickly reached & passed 100 degrees

It was all a bit scary because I felt like the city was expecting an aerial raid
But as I looked at conversing strangers I saw that friends were being made
I thought people would begin to panic worse than a repetitively light flashed iris
But I soon found myself talking to someone about a current computer virus

The train's cars were steamed up as everyone was sweating by the gallons
Some people wanted to strangle the mayor like a fish caught in an eagle's talons
We were told three hours later that we would be escorted through the subway tunnel
As people crowded the train's rear door looking like they were going through a funnel

The tunnel was dark and dirty as my clothes were in a wet soaked grunge
As I surfaced from the tunnel I felt just like the world's first human sponge
Two good looking women asked me for directions to the Port Authority station
But at that moment I didn't even know my own current location

Then one of them asked me if I could give her three dollars
As New York City's background was filled with confusion and taxi hollers
They were from Connecticut and in my condition I didn't know if it was a state or a sport
So the fare less woman credited my knowledge by saying that I was stupid and also short

It doesn't matter because I'm human and therefore subjected to imperfections
Besides, since I was in a state of shock I unwillingly gave her the wrong directions
So I got even with her subconsciously, as a dry journey home caused my throat to chafe
And after I got home; a cold shower never felt better, because for the most part, I was safe

We were stuck! All of us in that train knew what sardines in a can baking in an oven felt like on that day.

The Bond Of Our Love

With the bond of our love we can see this tough time through
Few words can describe the emotions I feel whenever I think of you
Even though we are apart because I am in this jail
I still want to uncover your face from underneath a veil

Everything I see that life has to offer is found in you
My waiting heart is like a drying flower longing for morning's dew
I close my eyes and inhale deeply to take in every ounce of air
I can't wait to lose myself inside your arms and womanly care

At this point my heart tears just as easily as clothing rips
But it quickly mends together when I think about your lips
Couples feel better because their love and everything else is shared
But the truth is that the mind and heart work better when they are paired

I need your love to live my life up to its fullest potential
If I had to think of one word to describe you, it would be "essential"
You are still the woman for me, and you are the one that I most desperately need
Please wait for me because the next time we meet, we will plant love's eternal seed

The Dark Poet

He is always wearing a black coat, black pants, and black shoes
The dark poet writes his eccentric, but yet rhythmic grooves
Writing is the only way he escapes the stress of a world gone mad
Never overlooking the hidden power of a pen and a pad

His tears can turn the generators found in hydroelectric plants
And when they fall they are concealed in the darkness of his pants
Some people forget the past and push forward like a fleet of fishing boats
Like them he has been there, done that, but went back to take some notes

Never forgetting some experiences and conquering emotions that made him kneel
He has the ability to look at someone's face and know exactly how they feel
Able to transfer his pain into words and onto a plain sheet of a notepad's paper
Releasing the demons within his soul like boiling water's steamy vapor

The dark poet is always dressed in black because his pain feels like a curse
But he lifts the darkness bit by bit with each line and rhyming verse
Though the darkness regenerates so quickly that it seems it might never go away
And for this darkened poet a clearing sky means that it turns from black to gray

The Driving Machines Behind A Man

Here is to all those hypocritical and materialistic thinkers
The ones who'd probably bow down if they saw "L.E.D." blinkers
The same people who say that they don't have a vehicular affinity
Until they see a man rolling up in a Mercedes Benz or Infiniti

I would look at my watch, and I tell you that three seconds is all it took
For an eye to look at an eighty thousand dollar car with an envying look
The people who spoke fiercely to a man before will now speak oh so gently
Because not too long ago they saw him appear from a nice & shiny Bentley

OH! And when a man suddenly shows up in a gleaming silver Audi?
All accents turn Texan because the first thing that's said is "howdy"
Women who never gave him the time or day now want to jump in the sack
Because they just love the "cushiony" foreplay of a Lincoln or Cadillac

If necks were made of glass then shatters would be heard around a block
As an attention robbing glow is given off by a man's Acura or Maybach
Let us not forget those who see money as similar as a plate of fettuccine
They will be the first to greet a man who is exiting a Bugatti or Lamborghini

Only with a great large income will cars connect in a daily nexus
And when a week begins with a BMW, and then ends with a Lexus
That is when guys want to "hang out" and women reveal their favorite "baking" pan
The moment they all bare witness to the driving machines behind a man

The Girl I Need

She's someplace in this world and she is the kind of girl I need
The one who'll take care of my loneliness problem, and heal me when I bleed
She will talk to me until the words coming from her phone start distorting
From her being so tired of speaking to me from yesterday's night into today's morning

She will never say that I am pessimistic
Because she knows my heart is just being realistic
She'll spare me the silence that brings isolation
By starting a cool topic for an interesting conversation

Because some women you'd talk to won't say nothing at all
And the words that you pitch at them come back like a bouncing ball
It's annoying to sit with them in groups because they stand out like a scared apprentice
And they go along with everyone else when things sound petty or momentous

The girl I need wouldn't be that way
She'll always be creative and have something to say
The kind of girl that I have to find
Will hold me tight and love me blind

The girl I need won't mind working a job that pays minimum wage
And she'll take good care of herself and get better with age
She'll look at me and give me her undivided attention
And fill me with all her warm and delicate affection

She will hold my hand and put her fingers between mine
Then she'll kiss me and tell me that she will love me for all time

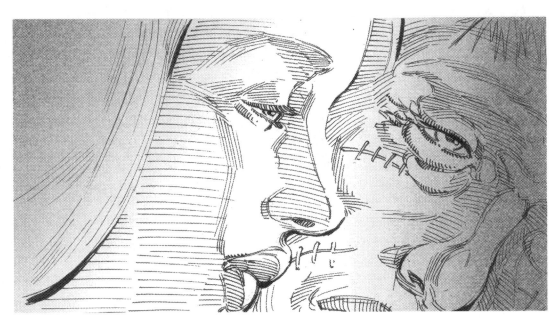

The Illness

Like any young person I want my life to rise and really soar
But something happened to me that changed my life back in 1994
I used to stab and puncture my lips with the wires from my braces
And now something grows on them that boggle the minds of medical aces

By doing that habit I would inflict the pain I needed to relieve my stress
But now I have an unknown illness and of my life it has made a mess
Hardened scab like skin grows on my lips, but occasionally it detaches
And it's difficult to accept the human body's unusual healing patches

I've tried many doctors, but the majority of them failed the quiz
When I ask them, "what's this condition?" and they don't know what it is
Some suggest a biopsy because my case is so bizarre
But it reveals nothing and I am left with a painful scar

I get so angry that I'll try crazy treatments, and some considered sane
I will never forget this one doctor's appointment that later gave me so much pain
If hell was a drink I gulped it down without first tasting it with a sip
Once the total of three steroid filled syringes were injected right into each lip

Without anesthesia I felt the whole inch of those needles as they startled every nerve
I was so mad at myself that I absorbed it all without a scream or a swerve
The dermatologist felt kind of sorry for me as he dried the tears that overflowed
My eyes looked like swimming pools, filled with the pain they couldn't hold

I wondered if the doctor thought that I was some kind of cyborg or android
But anesthesia wasn't applied because it would've counteracted with the steroid

Other doctors gave me promising theories, and some that were outrageous
But one good thing they all found out was that this thing is not contagious
The little social life that I once had was utterly destroyed
And the conversations that I loved so much I now had to avoid

I feel like a crow that will eat the seeds a farmer has just planted
As those seeds are all the little things that I always took for granted
I'm afraid to speak to people because I read their body language as they wonder
If my lips are always dry that way or if I'm dying of raving hunger

While people were in school learning why some angles are obtuse
I was scared to leave my home, so I was branded a recluse
Everyone else's life seemed to turn like a spinning windmill
When I faced myself I soon felt as if my life was standing still

My family wouldn't really notice it and they would miss every single clue
To be able to kiss someone is the one thing that I can't wholeheartedly do
Everyday I see people and cars go by as I watch them from my windowsill
You know, the world sure looks different whenever you are ill

The Life Of A Poem

It often has the simple words that are sometimes spoken by mothers
Engulfing a reader with angry thoughts or gentle loving smothers
Usually reaching a climax halfway down the middle
The way the most heat is generated at the center of a griddle

The life of a poem is short and its goal is to leave an impact when it expires
But after the first reading it often fades away and then retires
Much like a person, it wishes to live long and be remembered
Wanting to be noticed by everyone when its stanzas are dismembered

It loathes the sometimes sarcastic cliché of being called, "nice"
It's like a crow wanting fresh corn but having to settle for plain old rice
These are the days in which the life of a poem ends like a shirt that's made of cotton
When it is given a try and it feels good but later discarded and then forgotten

The Love I Feel

Please lay your head on my chiseled manly chest
And listen as my heart reveals that your love is the best
When I am with you my heart sees a beautiful inviting scene
And the sound that it generates is its loving theme

Whenever I look at you my heart beats very fast
Because it is running for your love that it knows will surely last
I cherish every single moment that we are together
And one minute that I'm not with you seems like forever

I gaze at your hands and I can instantly feel their entrancing spell of softness
They have the power to put any manic wild beast into a state of calmness
Your feet are kissably clean, and I want to soothe them with creamy warm milk
They are so smooth that when I touch them; it's as if though I am feeling silk

One look into my passionate eyes and I am sure you'd foresee
That the love I feel from you means everything to me
You have no idea how long I have waited to hold someone like you in my arms
My loneliness was like a group of stinging bees that always followed me in swarms

My sense of being is awakened from your feminine perfume that smells so sweet
And all the while my heart is feeling it all with each strong pulsating beat
Every time you make your love known to me it brings great joy and pleasure
"The amount of love that I feel for you?" No word on Earth can measure

For every part of my body that is both a solid and a liquid
Yearns for your female aura that is beautiful and so vivid
Come close to me so I may breathe in your luscious tasteful breath
As we kiss I feel empowered, as my loneliness meets its death

The Man From Her Dreams

A woman wants the man from her deepest, most secretive dreams
One who would massage her body with warm penetrating creams
A man that will give her all those deep conversations she would crave
The one who would be her life's partner and undying romantic slave

She wants him to cuddle her in his arms with the utmost delight
And look into her absorbing eyes with little fear or fright
Yes, she is certain that she wants that type of guy
Whose heart stays when his mouth says, "good-bye"

His promises would be like gold when she sees that they were all kept
And in bed he would be strong, and not sexually inept
He could make her fluids flow like gentle rivers or screaming falls
Whenever his hot passion enters her body and expands her vaginal walls

That dreamy man wouldn't tell her words that would start a confrontation
Instead he would build a relationship, and support it with love's foundation
He would know that she would want all of this, but as real as he would seem
She'd wake up with a racing pulse wishing he was factual, and not a dream

She'd wash her face to make sure she woke up, still believing he could never be true
Once she closed her sink's faucet, that man was somewhere; done washing his face too

The New Life

After September 11th, 2001 Americans opened up their eyes
And saw their vulnerability through a crazy terror guise
So now, a post 9/11/01 era, the new life that everyone now leads
People growing apart like stars when we were once closer than beads

Profiling other people for their religion, and hating those that wear a turban
Intoxicated with anxiety and panic attacks as if veins now flowed with bourbon
This new life is difficult to fathom, but oh so much harder to accept
Because 9/11/01 was so hard to believe, but true in all eyes as they wept

Now we glance behind our backs and fear that unattended bags have a hidden peril
We now wash foods more than twice, just to make certain that they are sterile
We're hoping someone doesn't have a body strapped bomb underneath a giant coat
We wish to live in medieval times again, because every important building had a moat

This new life is noticeable on shaking hands after a car's random backfire
It is felt in the Arabic shops that are no longer trusted by a loyal buyer
It's seen on the faces that spot a misplaced piece of clay
The word life is now an acronym for: Living In Fear Everyday

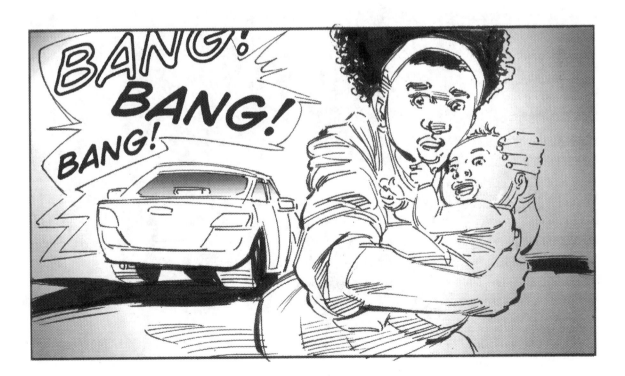

I admire it when I see it being driven or when it is in park
Its acceleration is legendary and just as fast as a spark
It is an extension of myself, a true mechanical reflection of my heart and soul
Bridge fare collectors get so entranced by its lines that they accidentally pay the toll

Even though the same car is made by Nissan's "Infiniti"
It just isn't the same when I get at a close proximity
Being inside and just the motion of turning the ignition key
Can transform any bad face into one that reflects glee

The sweetest sound is the one that emanates from its free revving V6
That makes people wonder if it has any kind of aftermarket tricks
Its instrument cluster mesmerizes me when it shines a red and black
It found its own path instead of following the usual automotive pack

I get so hypnotized when I walk passed it that I come close to taking a spill
I always strive to get in front of it at night so that I can see its lights and grille
I often dream of it waiting to rescue me from a boring work day like a hero
If anyone ever asks me what other car compares to it I will happily say, "ZERO!"

My prior 1998 Sage Mist Green Nissan Maxima

The Poem Speaks

Do not worry if I caused the greatest aggravation
Or if I sound dull because I have no punctuation
Just say me
Or write me
Do anything except fight me

I come from a deep place like a burying mole
And I come forth wanting to fulfill one goal
To allow them to know exactly how you feel
To tell them what you went through, yes, every ordeal

Tell me like I am no matter if some parts are sick and gory
For there is no such thing as each line being happy in every story
Don't ruin me with strict technique or semi-plagiaristic metaphors
I want to stand out like a meat eater inside a group of herbivores

Just say me
Or write me
But please don't deny me

Allow me to come in and possess your hand
Letting it flow like an hourglass filled up with sand
Speak the words or shout them out with courage and no fear
Because when you finish all will rise and for you they will all cheer

Listen, for I am your poem, yes I am alive and yes I speak
For you I'd ring victory bells or sound a painful but learning retreat
Open me up and watch me enter a pool of hearts with the most outstanding dive
I'll tell them how you went into life's hell, and then made it out alive

Just say me
Or write me
Please, visualize me!

The Strength For Him From Her

Baby? Do you still think of me as a man? Even though I am crying on your shoulder?
I feel pinned down with no where to go because of depression's heavy boulder
Please help me to make it through another overwhelming depression phase
Happiness is somewhere in my heart, but I need help guiding it through the maze

Depression makes me feel too lazy to go out and too worthless to do something
It tells me that my life will ultimately fade away and all I do will be for nothing
It asks me, "Why have fun when it always comes to an end?"
And, "Why receive the things that you yourself don't even send?"

I'm sorry I ruined the plans that we made to go out
I'm sorry for always feeling tired and not wanting to walk about
I'm sorry you now feel bad after you were so ecstatic
I'm sorry if you think that I am far way too dramatic

Sweetheart, now is when I think of you as a real man and I understand
I am always willing to talk to you with ease and not demand
You can count on me to break you out of any depressive daze
My heart will be the guiding beacon through the labyrinth's haze

I want you to know that life practically travels in fair and unfair warps
And I would much rather be a dead someone than a rotting unknown corpse
The best thing about having fun is the feeling you get from its initial start
And you should view everything that you obtain like a star on a progress chart

I'll say that it's okay as I touch your disappointed face
I'll give you strength with a warm and loving embrace
I am happier when I feel the energy that makes you so charismatic
I will only think that way if I see you acting as Shakespeare's Hamlet in the attic

These Women

So many beautiful women these days with such unbelievable bodies
I often feel like every corner store is now offering Pilates
These women convert my middle aged hormones into those of a boy in his teens
It's a coincidence to see them often in a New York City borough called, "Queens"

Because queen is the only word that comes close to their persona
The only thing missing is a justified crown with a surrounding corona
I love it when these women show off their immaculate feet with sandals
They are the wishes of every man who blows out his birthday candles

These women seem to enjoy doing one thing that can only be called a tease
When they pass me so closely & make their clean scent be carried by a breeze
My admiration for their beauty grows whenever their lips sport the color pink
I begin to cry like a baby because my eyes are locked and refuse to blink

In my opinion, I believe that these women who walk the Earth are God's gift to men
And the best thing a man ever did was asking God for these women way back then

Thinking About Death

I'm standing on this platform looking at all of these souls
Each one of them possesses short and long term goals
But I think to myself, "Who among them will continue living and who will die?"
And will they be cool in heaven's ocean or go to hell where they will fry

I look at every single one of them as I now ride on the train
Some faces look angry while others look distant and plain
Do they know that death is coming, and could be here any minute?
Tipping over their cup of life as it finally reached its limit

No, I doubt that they are thinking about that right now
Death is seeing us as fallen snow as it brings about its plow
Everyone might be healthy now so they won't imagine such a thing
But the grim reaper could be an approaching truck, or a bee's potential sting

Life is constantly moving forward with each day, because there's no turning back
Until it stops at that inevitable time when eye sights fade to black
I do just like everyone else as I tend to ignore death's coming wrath
But I do that because deep inside I feel it is clearing someone else a path

Thought She Was Reserved

Now that you saw her married & with a life, what did you really think?
That she'd wait for you to contact her with a letter written in loving ink?
Sorry brother, but love in this world adopts the rule, "First come first served"
She took the best rendition of her ideal man without knowing she was reserved

Or so, reserved was actually something that you'd make yourself think
So did her lover but he took a glass, picked up a spoon & made a clink
While you limited yourself with fears that you felt impossible to transcend
Her man made the toast of his beginning as it was the toast of your end

You looked at her and saw that beyond those fears were love & future marriage
How I wish you never did "she loves me she loves me not" with a head of cabbage
Because a flower gives you lesser chances & brings you to your senses quicker
But now her heart feels the result of a "just married" trunk and bumper sticker

This is the worst thing you ever did as you actually thought she was reserved for you
That's like leaving soup in front of starving people, assured that no one will eat that stew
I know that fear of rejection, prolonged loneliness, & fervid heartache makes you sad
But how about this now overwhelming feeling of losing something you could've had?

Thug

What is it that makes a person become a thug?
Could it be because their parents never gave them a hug?
I guess that is why thugs have peculiar greetings
Whenever they see each other or hold special meetings

With the way they act, who can take them serious?
To some people they appear frightening and hideous
Some thugs go as far as having gold plated teeth
And walk around with knives in a leather laced sheath

Most are uneducated because they dropped out of school
It's a gang's secret tradition and initiating rule
All the worst emotions that they keep inside
Feels as strong as two worlds ready to collide

All this time I was thinking serious wrongs
Now I know the theme behind rap songs
I thought that music was mostly about sex, violence and material idolatry
Then I saw rap's hidden acronym in the form of, "**R**hythmic **A**llegro **P**oetry"

The symbol of peace is the sight of a dove
And that is what they mean when they say, "One love"
I thought they were malicious people caught up in their greed
"Chilling" on the street corners and always smoking "weed"

It turns out however, that this is not always the case
As I talked to one and looked directly at his face
He told me about his school days and how he was a mathematician
And when he was in English class he knew words by definition

He scratched his braided hair as it began to itch
I noticed the scar on his right eye soon begin to twitch
All my negative thoughts now began to vanish
As he kept talking to me and saying things in Spanish

I shook his hand then I turned and departed
The words that he spoke were not for the fainthearted
The lesson I relearned from talking to that brother
Was to never judge a book by the look of its cover

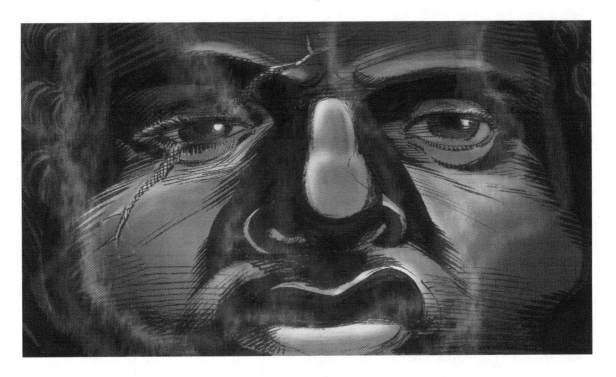

If these people look like thugs to me, then I have
to wonder what I must look like to them.

Thursday, June 17th, 2004...a day that I will never forget
I finally caught her with my heart's wanting net
There she was, my high school crush, going up a flight of stairs to take a train
I was driving my car & about to turn right when I was suddenly hit by my brain

The synapse: "OH MY GOD, THIS IS IT.....GO GET HER!!!!!"
I put that car in reverse as I shouted, "YESSSS SIR!!!"
God, you are so merciful and gracious, I thanked you for what happened next
Everything was happening so right that it actually left me perplexed

I called her name, but she didn't hear me. Oh my goodness! I didn't know what to do!
Then as if by divinity an old guy touches her shoulder and says, "Hey, he's calling you"
There I was...finally looking into her beautiful eyes
She's so beautiful, as she stood there looking so wise

She said, "hello" and kissed me on the cheek—I almost fainted from the emotion
The first thing I thought about was that my life was finally being set into motion
I actually touched her hand and it was so soft and tepid
I then offered her a ride home and she gratefully accepted

Oh God, it felt so good to have her right by my side
As she was enjoying the nice and very courteous ride
We exchanged contact information on two halves of a torn paper
As it soon turned into a large and very mysterious caper

She exited my car & dropped my contact information while leaving
My mind went into a spin through its sharp perceiving
It thought, "Did she drop it by accident or on purpose?"
"Did she consider it to be an expendable surplus?"

My emotions were in the sky because that's where they all soared
I contacted her with the info she gave me, but only to be ignored
At first I was happy and skipping like the child who sung, "A-tiskit-a-tasket"
But I quickly realized that I lost my heart along with the yellow basket

I guess the halve of the torn paper she gave me was like a premonition
Maybe she was showing the future of my heart after the surprising demolition
My God, is this the ending of this crush? The one that you already chose?
I guess so because now I see her as nothing more than a <u>bitter rose</u>

I have never ran up stairs as fast as I did on this day, but all for nothing.

To every poet his or her own
Satisfied reader by the sound of their moan
Because the words made the person feel so well connected
As a soul was either getting rebuilt or dissected

To every poet his or her own
Writing in the darkness all alone
Being engulfed by emotions like foods in acidic enzymes
Starting lines with free verse and then finishing with end rhymes

To every poet his or her own
Pain more excruciating than a broken bone
A feeling of lemon and salt being rubbed on a freshly opened wound
But that's the risk of trying to find real love in a world that's cartooned

To every poet his or her own
People telling them which skills to hone
Because technique is everything to them instead of being unique
Those people never give compliments, just lots of critique

To every poet his or her own
Person who despises or loves a writer unknown
The same way a sunbather is either disappointed or ecstatic with their tan
To every poet his or her own biggest hater or tremendous fan

To My School Teachers

Before going to you, my life was a book with deep encryptions
But you made it clearer with your own unique descriptions
Sometimes you made me so mad that I thought my top was going to explode
But that was just one of your many ways to get me into a learning mode

With repeating words and phrases you literally pounded brains into submission
But you knew that the only way to learn was through countless repetition
You strived to make every student special, and at the same time make them equal
When you allowed some to pass your class and made others go through a sequel

You pointed out my talents to my blind folded parents with a good cause
For the biggest tragedy is to be known as, "The star that never was"
With books you taught me knowledge, but discipline came with attendance sheets
Because you know that a mind would last longer than a muddy pair of cleats

Your bravery was incredible when you took over forty minds with such authority
As you weren't scared to break out into your own from tough conformity
If it weren't for you, I would still be sucking my thumb, questioning my existence
I want to thank you for the teachings and for being here to make a difference

To The Hating Critics

When you finish reading my book I bet you'll say, "I wasted time reading this crap"
How you'll think, "People won't want to read the book of this poor depressing sap"
Yes, I'm sure you will tell people not to get this book once you write your review
Detesting it, and adding it to your list of books that are a waste of glue

Openly speaking; you'll criticize my published dream come true
Nevertheless, I am so convinced that this is what you'll do
'cause it's okay, say what you feel, it is your job to address
The public of things they might like, and the things that won't impress

Yawning at my work you'll give it a rating of one out of five stars
Or use it to keep your tables dry from wet or staining jars
Ultimately throwing away my book in a garbage can on the street
Kicking aside any hidden messages because you found out some words repeat

Insisting that there are things in my book no one else could possibly like
Saying that it doesn't make sense like when billion dollar companies go on strike
Suggesting that people skip this and give something else a try
My only question that I would ask of you is, "Why?"

You don't know if other people will like the things I have to say
But you'll persist that from this book they should simply stay away
Unmoved from my words you'll finish your review with a discouraging negative sign
There is something I would like to tell you for killing the one dream that was mine

Take the letters & punctuation mark from the start of every line & please combine

To The Reader

Hello reader, how are you? I want to apologize to you at this moment
I'm truly sorry if you thought my poems were senseless, or "not potent"
Have you ever wondered why the majority of people keep their feelings locked inside?
And how they walk around cool like Jekyll but deep down they feel like Hyde

What are we supposed to do with all of our feelings and emotions?
Drink them away with disgusting beers or crazy potions?
At one time I was deluged from what I felt, and was close to going berserk
But once I allowed my feelings to surface they arose with my greatest work

After analyzing the word poem, I saw it as an acronym, and I found out what it stood for
I believe that a poem **P**ours **O**ut **E**very **M**oment, and with words that seem to roar
Ever noticed the obvious hole left in a sheetrock wall after it was hit by a hammer?
That's the damage done to my soul if my feelings aren't converted to some type of grammar

Also, you might see some lines in my poems without a period or a semi-colon
Because they would rob the end-rhymed timing faster than a bike being stolen
Like the naked body that uses clothing to prevent indecent exposure
I use this kind of poetry to bring myself a sense of closure

If you decide to return my book I won't be shocked or stunned
You have the right to go back to the store and ask for a prompt refund
But before you treat my book like a supermarket's shopping cart
Please sit someplace where you can be alone, and reread it with your heart

Today's Job Market

(Last) I thought that a degree guaranteed its holder a future with profound success
    And that struggling with local paths was better than riding the ones going express

I could have sworn that a job market meant, "Take your pick from a huge variety"
Not, "Take whatever comes your way so you don't get unemployed anxiety"

(Second) Women are now getting better jobs, but only because of an attractive appearance
    And then honored later for their fantastic skills and unmatched coherence

The job market of today has never been so throat cutting competitive
Yet the tasks involved have become easier due to the work being repetitive

(#1) We are living in a society where people who don't even have a G.E.D.
    Are actually given jobs that require them to possess a four year degree

There was a time in which having a degree meant that you had a uniquely colored glow
But in today's job market knowledge is last, looks are second, and #1 is who you know

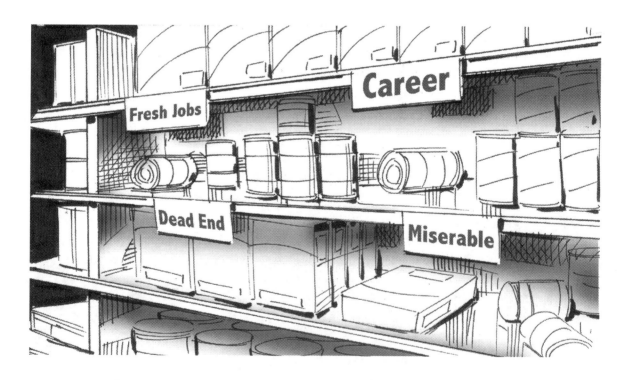

U.S. Armed Forces

SO! You're tired of being soft and looked at as a wimp?
You say that everyone compares your size to a little baby shrimp?
Hey, we'll make you so hard that your teeth could open up a can of sardines
You'll be one of the few and the proud, come join the Marines!

You notice that your life isn't exactly taking flight
And admit that you're scared of every single height
Enlist with us and your future will be straight instead of wavy
We'll make you want to climb high, become a part of the Navy!

Youths have a problem; they don't take life serious
And when push comes to shove; they give up and get delirious
They love to stay home to play video games or dream of dating a Ken or Barbie
This unit can make them stand confident & mature, think about the Army!

You look to the sky and sigh because you're aching to be on a winning team
You long for friends that can help you through fire and burning steam
Look no further because stars are the guiding lights for this course
We'll push you beyond the sky, your place is here...in the Air Force!

You can't believe how the world is today with so much harsh injustice
And how peace & freedom seem further away than the sun in a Winter solstice
You can do something about it and help heal the hearts that have been marred
We'll make you able to go anywhere water flows, sign up for the Coast Guard!

Think before you throw your life away scraping dung in a local zoo
And realize a future with your country, for Uncle Sam wants YOU!
Make your inner power known like a stampede of wild horses
Become better than you've ever been, in the U.S. Armed Forces!

What Will Truly Become Of Me?

Sometimes I wonder, "What are people truly going to think of me?"
"Are they going to describe my poems as dirty laundry or potpourri?"
Will people see me as a very well known poet or forgettable rotting rubbish?
Will someone say that I stole the poem they never had time to copyright or publish?

I wonder if one of my poems will win me a much decorated prize
Or allow someone to romance their significant other while watching the sun rise
Will I be included in the long list of great writers under the title of, "Creatively truthful poet?"
Will my last name's pronunciation be debated like a French wine's case of mo-aye vs. mo-wett?

Will my writings be good enough for the world's most renowned scholars?
Or be interesting enough to be recommended to waiting women in beauty parlors?
Will a poem of mine change a part of someone's life as one of the end results?
Are people going to worship me and form dedicated poetic cults?

Will teachers look at all my poems and take one as a sample?
To say that it was excellent writing or an idea of a bad example?
I wonder if anyone will misunderstand me for anything that I proclaim
Well, whatever happens I will continue living and loving just the same

Why I Show My Love

I continue to be kind, despite the awful things some people do to me
I say, "I'm sorry" when it should really be the other person's apology
I find no reason to fight for the simple act of two bumping shoulders
For it is better to be called a coward than amass crime recording folders

Besides, it really wouldn't matter if something was done or not
Because in one hour or the next day, both parties would have forgot
That is why I show my love, even though it can be difficult to do in a harsh situation
For diarrhea of mouths is less effective than linguistic constipation

If a man married a woman from any U.S. city, or from a place as far as Galilee
They wouldn't be seen as anything else now but two people starting a family
That is why I show my love, because we're all united from the color of our blood
What about culture? Hey, every type of flower had to have come from a single bud

I'm holding something back, and the aforementioned means little compared to one thing
For I have seen death snatch baby birds from under their mother's protective wing
The true reason why I show my love to everyone, without EVER trying to mask it
Is because things get so different, when I hear that a person is now lying in a casket

Writer's Block

What the heck am I doing reading a soup can's label?
Why am I beating around the bush when I am ready, willing, & able?
Damn this inevitable thing called, "writer's block"
My hand is like an idling boat waiting at an empty dock

I hear everything in the form of a ticking clock
Nothing helps, not even the position of the thinker on a rock
Maybe if I lie down on my bed I'll lose it before I fall asleep
NO! WAKE UP! It's taking a shot that is really cheap!

I had such a good line too, but unfortunately, I got writer's block
Maybe a static discharge from my rug can kill it from the shock
Perhaps if I pretend I'm going out it'll leave before I put on my socks
OH NO! There it is at the door! Unfastening all the locks!

Let's see if it can swim once I go take a shower
With a green apple soap that smells really sour
Great! I dropped the slippery bar like a nervous daydreaming dope
Or is writer's block doing this to get behind me once I reach for the soap?

It is so overwhelming, I almost feel like a swimming zebra being targeted by a croc
Let's find out what a dictionary says about this, "Writer's block"
"A paralyzing phase that distorts literary ideas & keeps them from flowing as they wood"
As they wood? Don't they mean express conditionally or possibility? A.K.A. "would"

Oh wait, the dictionary just secretly clued me in on how to eliminate this writer's block
By telling me that it is made up of a hard fibrous substance that is plentiful in stock
That means that its biggest enemy would be a persistent little wood eating mite
But in my case, I need to gnaw away at it with each letter that I write

Your Male

I'm not here to call you names that sound derogatory
My vow was to protect you in known & unmarked territory
You'll have my support no matter if you succeed or fail
I am your brother, your guardian, your father, your male

I entered this world to complete your aura
To turn your life from a tundra into a flora
To make your life more effervescent than ginger ale
I am your son, your nephew, your darling, your male

I'm with you through the easy things & the hardest works
I'll enter your deepest cavern where an orgasmic feeling lurks
I'll be your sunbathing spot or shelter from falling hail
I am your husband, your lover, your rock, your male

Mixing with you is in my chemistry from morning to dusk
My essence attracts you with a deep hard smelling musk
I can make things sweet again after you thought they were stale
I am your testosterone, your masculinity, your sugah, your male

To our females,

Know and understand that we will always be these
things to you for as long as we exist.

Quotes

"While it is true that, 'All that glitters isn't gold,' but, what if it was gold and you lost the chance to obtain it because you were afraid to feel like a fool if it wasn't?"

-Raymond A. Hiraldo

"You were designed for a particular mate that would be attracted by your entirety. If you change too drastically then, you run the risk of missing that one soul mate; practically designed for you."

-Raymond A. Hiraldo

"Feelings and emotions are the most confusing & difficult things to understand, no words could ever get them right, they can only come close."

-Raymond A. Hiraldo

"Another experience in capture equals another page, and if that same experience is made into a chapter then it will calm the hardest rage."

-Raymond A. Hiraldo

"Sometimes your deepest pain can surface bringing with it your greatest work."

-Raymond A. Hiraldo

"Be careful with kindness, for just because someone is kind to you doesn't necessarily mean that they like you."

-Raymond A. Hiraldo

"Physical pain is nothing compared to the pain that's felt inside"

-Raymond A. Hiraldo

"Certain things in life can be difficult, but never impossible."

-Raymond A. Hiraldo

"If a woman was like a field of corn and if a man was like a crow, then, a man needs to brave a woman's scarecrow in order to enjoy her crops."

-Raymond A. Hiraldo

Quotes

"There is no way you will be able to sell yourself to a potential mate if you don't consider yourself to be goods."

-Raymond A. Hiraldo

"While it is true that 'the way to a man's heart is through his stomach,' but, the way into his heart's force is through his mind. For the more he thinks of you, then, the more his heart will beat for you."

-Raymond A. Hiraldo

"There is no question that 'Curiosity killed the cat' but, I believe that curiosity buried it too."

-Raymond A. Hiraldo

"If your creativity feeds off of negativity then, you will be creative for the rest of your life."

-Raymond A. Hiraldo

"If I am seeking the attention of an individual or the world, and if I obtain that attention through humility then, have I really humiliated myself if I got what I wanted?"

-Raymond A. Hiraldo

"Sometimes it is better to spend more time trying to be present than looking like one."

-Raymond A. Hiraldo

"Sometimes we'll 'love' the wrong person so that we can be made more aware of what we're capable of doing to/with the right person."

-Raymond A. Hiraldo

"A person who tries to hold a lot, grips little."

-Raymond A. Hiraldo

"It makes no sense in moving forward if you have no 'forward' to move on to"

-Raymond A. Hiraldo

Acknowledgements

I'd like to use this final area for just a few more words to express my gratitude. I really want to thank God again for giving me this opportunity. There have been so many times in which I could have been fatally hurt in my life, but God was always there to spare me.

On a more positive note, it is kind of funny that my initials spell, "RAH." So I am sure that the completion of my destiny to publish this book is making a lot of angels in heaven shout, "Go Raymond, Go Raymond, RAH! RAH! RAH!" A sense of humor is always good, right? A huge thank you goes out to Trafford for publishing me.

The following list is just a few "thank yous" that I really needed to send out.

Lydia D. Capellan — a mother who always worked so hard to get me into the right things

Alejandro A. Hiraldo — a father who pushed me beyond what I was capable of

Domingo A. Canela Jr. — a true <u>best</u> friend who stood by me when no one else wanted to

Robin Small McCarthy — an amazing teacher/friend who accepted me with so much love

Sarah Tay — a beautiful person with great support. I love the "backbone" Godiva

Candice Powell — a great family friend with lots of nurturing intelligence

Gisell N. Claudio (My #1 Po-G-Ter) — a lovely person with so much guidance, and care

Nissan Motor Co. — the only automotive company that actually has a vehicle with a soul

TCI-The College of Technology — a place that harbored all the energy I needed to awaken my inner writer

Cristobal Crespo — a person who led me to the opportunity I needed so that this whole crazy project could be funded. Thank you for believing in me as strongly as you did

Charles J. Denegall Jr. — a brilliant, understanding, hard working and caring person who was the best manager I have ever had the privilege to work with

George Baquero (www.georgebaqueroillustration.com) — an amazing illustrator who brought my ludicrous cover art idea & comical high school crush art idea to life

To all the women who rejected me I sincerely thank you all for the inspiration. While it can feel like a foot on the neck at times; negative energy is creatively powerful in the right hands.

To those of you who I've missed, who needs to have their name in a book anyway, right? Okay, okay! I'll get you the next time, if God instills it in my destiny.

And here is to my supporters/readers....

Thank You!

With lots of peace, love and happiness

Notes